NICE TO MEET YOU

NICE TO MEET YOU

JESSIE J

SIMON &
SCHUSTER

London · New York · Sydney · Toronto · New Delhi

A CBS COMPANY

First published in Great Britain by Simon & Schuster UK Ltd, 2012
A CBS COMPANY

Copyright © Jessie J / Who You Are Ltd, 2012

Simon & Schuster UK Ltd
1st Floor
222 Gray's Inn Road
London
WC1X 8HB

www.simonandschuster.co.uk

Simon & Schuster Australia, Sydney
Simon & Schuster India, New Delhi

A CIP catalogue record for this book is available from the British Library

ISBN: 978-1-47111-074-0

Reprinted November 2012

Designed and typeset by Ascetic Studios
Printed and bound in Great Britain by Butler Tanner & Dennis Ltd, Frome, Somerset

Nice To Meet You
Jessie J
with Hattie Collins

*I dedicate this book to
my mum and dad*

CONTENTS

CHAPTER ONE

MAMMA KNOWS BEST

'Mamma knows best when times get hard // And Papa always has a joke to make me laugh // See Mamma knows best when I feel down // To bring me up but always keep my feet on solid ground…'

Mamma Knows Best

From being born under a table to learning 'Twinkle, Twinkle, Little Star', my early years were full of adventure, fun and, most importantly, FAMILY.

NEW BEGINNINGS

Hello. I'm Jessica. Nice to meet you... *Waves*. On 27 March 1988 I was born under my mum and dad's bedside cabinet at home! Well, it was beneath the bed and the bedside table. I was born at 9.27am in the house I lived in with my mum, dad and two older sisters, until I was fourteen years old, in Seven Kings, Essex – right near Seven Kings station, down the scary alleyway. Dun dun duuuuun! *That's how I have always explained it*.

I was born with the umbilical cord around my neck, so I was really purple when I came out. My sisters, Hannah and Rachel, were both there – it was a full-on family experience. They were five and seven years old when I was born. They were in the bedroom, wondering if I was going to be a boy or a girl, because my parents didn't know what they were having.

My mum and dad decided on me being a home birth as both my sisters were born in hospitals. I think they just wanted to be at home so my mum could be comfortable.

There are pictures of me being born, but I don't think my mum would forgive me if I put them in this book!

I was named Jessica Ellen Cornish – Jessica after my nan's sister. Ellen because my mum and dad liked it I guess. My mum's middle name is Jessie, and so Jessie J being my stage name, it's nice that it still has a connection to family. To be honest, there's no real reason for the 'J' (always feel like I disappoint people when I say that). People always ask what it stands for, but the reason can change daily. Today it could be 'Jessie Joker' because I just made my friend laugh on the phone. *Creative*. It just sounded good and was... well, catchy. Today Jessica Cornish is the name I use as a songwriter and Jessie J is my name as a performer and singer.

My friends and family call me Jessica mostly. I still have to get used to people calling me Jessie sometimes.

I have in the past read that I am in fact from Redbridge, Chadwell Heath, Brighton... but I grew up in Seven Kings. Look at that: setting the facts straight right from the first chapter. BOOM!

I loved that house so much. It was a detached, four-bedroom house with a loft conversion. My sisters had the loft conversion and I was always so jealous because to me it was like living at the top of a castle. I had such a strong connection with the house because all my childhood memories were there and, obviously, I was born there. When my sisters moved out, the house felt far too big for just the three of us.

I suppose as a child you never think about moving house, I never did. Luckily, when we did, I didn't have to change school and I still got to see my friends, so it was just a matter of getting used to a new home and a new area. But I cried so hard the day we moved, I remember it clearly. Walking around saying goodbye to each room. Slightly dramatic. I'm sure I wore all black too. Weird.

Some of my earliest memories are of family holidays and days out with my parents and sisters. My dad would take me and my sisters swimming, and we would always go to Wimpy afterwards for chips and milkshakes. Even now when I go swimming I want chips and milkshakes afterwards. Standard. I had a really happy and adventurous childhood. If I think back to being little, I think of running around in the rain, stage school, sleepovers, adventures to London, camping in the garden *don't ask, it was to toughen us up* and Cornwall.

Cornwall is where we used to go on holiday every Easter. I think of my mum covering our coats in those bright yellow reflective stickers so we didn't get run over or lost – instead we kind of looked like miniature highlighter pens – and my dad would constantly be thinking of pranks to pull on us and making us laugh until we couldn't breathe. I also remember going to butterfly houses and Flambard's (best theme park ever).

There were a lot of sleepovers; my mum and dad always let me have friends stay. At the time it was normal for me to have friends over most Saturday nights. Now I am older I realise how generous my mum and dad were; how loving and giving they were to all my friends. We never had lots of money or the newest clothes but I never even really noticed. My mum and dad always made the best of what we could afford.

We'd go abroad to Corfu or Majorca once every five years maybe, but we'd go to Cornwall every year and stay in a caravan. I remember seven-hour car journeys being very cramped, walkmans fully charged; I really loved my word search book and also discussing ideas for the Easter bonnet parade. Very serious stuff. *Serious face*.

> **MY MUM AND DAD** decided on me being a home birth as both my sisters were born in hospitals.

Me singing in Mullion, in Cornwall.

"I NEVER STOPPED SINGING"

My first ballet exam.

ARIES ADVENTURES

The very first words I spoke were 'jam hot', from the Beats International song 'Dub Be Good To Me'. I was just over a year old apparently. My sisters would constantly sing it to me, so I just picked up on the easiest bit to sing back.

'Jaaaaaaaaaam hot!'

Although I loved singing and dancing when I was really young, art and acting were initially my main passions. I loved art and drawing and even now I find it relaxing to sit down and draw – it helps me focus my mind a bit and switch off from everything. I loved acting and playing a character. It was always so interesting to me, to step into the unknown and let all my inhibitions go and be someone else for a bit. Especially when I was younger and unwell, it would help me forget. They still fascinate me now – films, plays and character building. I was always singing and dancing because I genuinely loved to entertain and make people happy from a young age. I watch home videos, and I didn't ever stop running around, making whale noises, pretending to be a television. Normal child stuff? Maybe not.

I was very talkative, because I had two older sisters, so they would always be pushing me to learn. I was always in a rush to catch up with them – 'I wanna be a big girl', I used to say to my mum and dad. My sisters used to give me extra homework, so by the time I was six I could say the days of the week in French. Every 6-year-old needs to know that. LOL.

I never stopped singing – I sang everywhere I went. My first performance was when I was three years old, and I sang 'Twinkle, Twinkle, Little Star' on a tape recorder at a caravan park in Cornwall for a competition. I was wearing a purple knitted jumper and floral leggings and dolly shoes – so not too different from now. My sisters played the recorder and I went wrong – it was so embarrassing, even at the age of three I was aware I had messed up.

We lost to a 6-year-old who sang 'Lady In Red'. Bet he didn't know the days of the week in French though.

We also had a trio called The Three Cornish Pasties; I sang, Rachel played the trombone and Hannah played the piano. Our theme tune was 'We are the Cornish Pasties 1, 2, 3!' Oh we were cool. *Cringe*.

" WE PERFORMED MOSTLY IN MY MUM AND DAD'S LIVING ROOM ON A SATURDAY AFTERNOON "

We performed mostly in my mum and dad's living room on a Saturday afternoon, until we ventured to bigger venues such as my mum and dad's garden, singing to my uncles and aunts and my grandparents. We'd be in high-waisted jeans, black T-shirts and Ray-Bans – thinking about it now, my dress sense really has never changed. Who knows, maybe one day the trio will re-form? My sisters can be the support act on my tour. I would actually pay to see that.

We have footage of me dressed as 'Sid the Seagull' at the caravan park we went to in Cornwall. I started unwrapping Sid's magic torch, showing everyone that my mum had made it out of a toilet roll. Nothing was a secret with me when I was young, I was very honest, and that is definitely something that hasn't left me. I've always said exactly what I'm thinking, but I'm a pro at keeping secrets now.

You were either in the 'Sid the Seagull' or the 'Lizzie the Lizard' team in Cornwall, and we were always in the Sid team. I loved Sid, little did I know it was probably an 18-year-old in a hired seagull suit, but at the time it was magical. We went back there for our last family holiday, when I was about fourteen years old, and we were put in the Lizzie the Lizard team. *Shock horror*. We were so upset, well not really. It became an ongoing joke the whole holiday. Even now if something goes wrong we blame it on Lizzie. Bless Lizzie. My mum and dad had their honeymoon in Cornwall, so we'd always go specifically to Land's End, Penzance, Looe Bay and Mullion. My parents would tell us stories about what they did there when they were growing up.

Cornwall remains one of my favourite places in the world – it's just beautiful. It is a very special place to us as a family. We had so much fun on our holidays there. You had to make something out of nothing then, because there were no computer games or

BlackBerrys or Sky+. We'd pretend that a tree was a castle and the sticks were snakes trying to get us and my dad was a monster. My mum and dad were amazing, encouraging us to use our imaginations and play and sing and dance and draw.

I'm really close to my sisters. They were nearer in age to each other, though, and that much older than me, so when I was younger, I remember sitting and watching them do their make-up before going to see *The Rocky Horror Show* or a night out clubbing. I'd be really jealous that I couldn't go. They got to stay up later than me and could watch *Catchphrase*, though I think that was on at quarter past six, so who knows what time I went to bed! Clearly extremely early.

Rachel and I had a moon and stars bag, like something out of *Harry Potter*, which we stashed sweets in and hid from Hannah in the wardrobe. Seems so mean now, we only told her about it recently. Funny, she didn't mind. We basically spent all our money on sweets and chocolates and we'd share the stash and write down what we'd eaten. It's really weird what you do as a kid. I remember we also used to put random ingredients into a bowl and leave it under the radiator to see what happened over night. To me it was so scientific, in fact it was toothpaste and grass in a bowl.

I was four years old when my mum and dad told me I could start ballet class at my local dance school. I was so excited. The Wenn Stage School was at the end of our road (down the scary alleyway) in Seven Kings and I went there several times a week until I was twelve or thirteen years old. I started with ballet then went to tap and modern. I ended up being there every day doing everything, including drama, singing and jazz, the lot. I was very lucky to have parents who supported what I loved to do.

I was with KrackersKids Theatrical Agency while I was at Wenn. Through them, I was in the Nickelodeon adverts – 'Are you in', anyone remember that? I did *Inherit The Wind* at the Old Kings Head Pub in Islington and I got the part of Brat in *Whistle Down The Wind*, which I was in for two consecutive years, playing one of the child lead roles. Juggling school and shows was tough but I loved it. It was where I got my first taste of wanting to make performing my life. I was nine years old, so I was serious. Haha!

I also did The British Arts Awards – a competition where different dance schools from all over the country competed in various categories. I entered lots of categories, and acting and singing were the two I always got furthest in. I did a character piece once as a shoe shop assistant doing ballet, it was terrible. I should try and find the video and put it online, very embarrassing. The Wenn Stage School, I know, have put up some videos of me performing when I was younger on YouTube. One of me as Aladdin is classic. *Cringe*.

"MY MUM, ROSE, WAS A BALLET DANCER WHEN SHE WAS YOUNG"

"THERE WAS A LOT OF SOUL"

FAMILY TIES

We are quite a large family. My mum has four brothers and my dad has three brothers, so there are a lot of uncles, aunties and cousins, and lots of grandchildren.

My mum's father passed when I was about three, I remember his smile and him playing with me and my sisters a lot. I still have pictures of us. My mum's mum, my Nanny B, is amazing and is the reason I am obsessed with star signs and long pointy nails and the colour green.

My dad's mum also passed when I was three – it's so crazy how much I look like her. I saw a picture recently, and we have the same eyebrows and smile. My dad's dad, my granddad, is hilarious just like my dad, and an extremely talented drummer, and his wife, Nanny S, would always let me do her hair and make-up and give me treats.

My mum, Rose, was a ballet dancer when she was young and, looking at old photographs, our figures were exactly the same. My mum is now a primary school teacher and has been for almost twenty years. My dad, Steve, always wanted to be a comedian, he is 100 per cent the funniest person I know. He has been a social worker for almost twenty-five years. Both of my sisters were actresses growing up, they loved drama. My elder sister Hannah is now a professional photographer and married to Calum, with two beautiful children. Rachel is an amazing poet and married to Pete, with a gorgeous son.

My brothers-in-law, Calum and Pete, are the brothers I never had. They are the best and are so protective of me. We talk cars, music and films. Boy stuff. Grrrrr.

This is a bit embarrassing to admit, but we used to have 'family conference meetings' on Saturday afternoons, or if we'd all had a row. My dad and my mum would sit us down and say, 'Right, what's going on in your lives? Is there anything you need to talk about?'

We are a very open and honest family and as children we were taught that it's healthy to discuss your problems and feelings with people who love and care for you.

I didn't take for granted the fact that I had that growing up and still don't now. My mum and dad would always say, 'Put your nightmares on the shelf and your dreams on the table.' We'd sit and talk about everything for hours if needed and then put on some of our favourite music to cheer all of us up. James Brown, The Funkadelic, D. Train, Joan Armatrading, Bob Marley and Tracy Chapman. There was a lot of soul and funk played in our house growing up.

As I developed my own tastes, I listened to TLC and the Spice Girls. I always wanted to be Posh but always had to be Sporty. KMT. My sister Rachel was obsessed with Peter Andre, as well as old-school rap music, like Run-DMC. Hannah loved Take That. I remember one year she had a Take That cake, she still finds it funny now that I know Gary Barlow. Take That weren't my favourite band growing up; for me, it was all about 5ive. Music was always the thread running through us as a family coming together and being happy.

Me and my sisters at a family wedding. It had to be done!

PLAYGROUND DAYS

I went to Goodmayes Primary School in Goodmayes (obvs) where my mum was also a nursery school teacher. My sisters went there too and it was a great school. It's funny going back now and seeing how small it is, it felt huge when I was little, like a maze of endless fun. It was cool having my mum there as a teacher. The only time she embarrassed me was Red Nose Day. She had a Dipsy (the green Teletubby) bag, which she put a red nose on, and she walked through the school playground wearing it. I was just like, 'I'm so embarrassed.' Even now my friends say she was one of the best teachers they ever had – so caring and thoughtful, always putting others before herself.

Every report said: 'Jessica is a very intelligent child, she just needs to stop talking and stop distracting others.' I'd probably get the same assessment now, to be honest. I am professional but I have my moments where I just want to be silly.

I remember being at school once and pretending to be sick so I could be sent home, by chewing up a digestive biscuit and spitting it out. I remember thinking, 'Muhahaha, I've done it, I have fooled them all.' Then my mum came in and simply said, 'You've just chewed up a digestive biscuit, haven't you?' I was so embarrassed, because I'd blagged all of the people there but she just knew. Mums just know.

I played clarinet at primary school – badly. My mum wouldn't buy me new reeds if I didn't practise, so when I performed at the school assemblies, there I'd be, squeaking away. Trying to make it sound like some sort of clarinet remix.

We'd do this thing called 'Show and Tell', where you had to either bring something to show the class, tell a story, or perform a song or dance. My friend Hannah and I were meant to be doing a tap dance, but the teacher, Mrs Taffe, forgot about us. We sat in leotards and tap shoes at the back of the assembly hall with everyone looking at us, freezing cold. I don't remember the song, but I remember the dance. I can still do it!

I did more dancing at school than singing. I loved making up dance routines on the benches. I took it so seriously though – it's funny looking back. Me and my friend Holly, who is still my best friend now, did a dance to MN8's 'I've Got A Little Something For You', and in the performance she high-kicked so high that she hit herself in the face with her leg. Classic Holly.

I also remember being in the country dance club and going to Brownies. I loved doing the deeds to collect my badges and I'm sure I still have my satchel somewhere. One of my tasks to get a Brownie badge was to make a cup of tea. Sounds easy, but I knocked it over and burnt myself and had to be taken to A & E to get burn cream and huge clingfilm bandages that would show just how much I didn't deserve the badge. However, I was so excited that I had something dramatic to share with everyone at Show and Tell. I never got the badge. It's OK – you're allowed to laugh.

I grew up with a girl called Hashmi. She lived across the road from me and we did everything together, including Brownies. We wore the same clothes and spent all our time together. I have this vivid memory of us one time when it was snowing, and we were walking to school. We both had bobble hats on.

Me and Hashmi at Primary School.

I remember us, about seven years old, running down the street, shaking our heads and making the bobbles move. Even now when I wear bobble hats, I do that. It's funny how those things just stay with you. We were obsessed with Forever Friends – we had plates, mugs, outfits, lunchboxes. Everything.

Hashmi taught me Gujarati. I used to speak Gujarati a lot when I was younger and I wish I could still remember some now. She taught me songs and words to say and she would giggle sometimes because she would make me say rude words to her family and then I'd get into trouble. There are videos of me speaking and singing in Gujarati somewhere. Another one to find... :)

In primary school, I was loud and silly; like most of the other kids, I just wanted to blend in. I loved swinging on the climbing frame and I had a bright lime-green Ellesse tracksuit. I dressed quite tomboyish sometimes; I loved making up dance routines, but had no issue with playing football or doing sports. I remember once making my mum buy me a Cabbage Patch Kids doll because everyone had them, and when I went up to the girls who were playing with them they just laughed at me. I preferred Pokémon, marbles

EVERY REPORT SAID: Jessica is a very intelligent child, she just needs to stop talking and stop distracting others...

and conkers anyways.

Birthdays and birthday parties were something that my mum and dad always made special. I had sleepovers, a magician (who spat when he spoke, never forget him, he was no Dynamo), Kid's Kingdom, Al's Fun House (I lost my blue silk purse that had £60 in it. I left it on the ground in the car park and when we went back, amazingly, it was still there. I also remember that day I was wearing Adidas jogging bottoms, the ones that gave you electric shocks. Random.) I had a 70s themed party for my thirteenth and I wore a gold dress. I asked a boy to dance and he said, 'I'm allergic to gold.' I was devastated. I was so much taller than all the boys. It was never easy. LOL.

One year I had a Goresbrook party (it was a leisure centre). I remember it was boiling hot and Holly and me were outside doing a dance routine – I was wearing blue flares. (It just gets worse.) I was ten, and me and Holly were running around, when we found a guy who had passed out from taking drugs. His dog was licking his face as he lay around the side of the leisure centre. I remember running back as fast as I could to tell an adult. The ambulance men said we probably saved his life.

"THERE ARE TIMES WHEN I KEEP MYSELF TO MYSELF, AND I'M NOT OUT THERE BEING LOUD, AND THAT'S HOW I WAS IN HOSPITAL"

My head shot from when I auditioned for
Whistle Down The Wind.

A CHANGE OF HEARTBEAT

I was around seven years old when I first got ill. I've got an irregular heartbeat. My dad has Wolff-Parkinson-White syndrome, so he was always great at explaining what it was I was feeling when I first started to experience it.

I've never liked being kept in the dark when it comes to health. If I'm going to get sick, tell me. If someone's ill, tell me. If my results are not normal, tell me; ever since I was young I have liked to know what is going on, so I can prepare and be strong to deal with it, however minor or major it is. It's important to always remain positive.

My health isn't as bad now as it once was, no way near. But there are still moments when I have to make sure I'm looking after myself and not pushing myself too hard. I have to be realistic; I don't want to push myself so much that I have to take two years out afterwards. Just like everyone else, I have to rest my body and my mind from time to time.

The very first time something happened was when we were in Epping Forest. For some reason, when I think of

Me and my best friend Holly, having a day out at Hamleys, when I first fell ill. :)

that day, I think of Wotsits! I don't know why, whether I ate them or what, but my clearest memory of that day is a packet of Wotsit crisps.

We were going back to the car after a day out and my dad said, 'Race ya', so we started running but I collapsed. Because I could be quite dramatic and silly, even back then, my dad thought I was just messing about. But I couldn't move and I couldn't breathe. My dad realised it was serious, so he picked me up and we drove to the hospital. I was afraid and confused. Weird when you're fine and then all of a sudden something like that happens and you don't know why, it can be terrifying.

The worst thing when you've got a heart problem is having to do running tests with only a bra on when you're just starting puberty. Sounds ridiculous, but I used to get more nervous about that than anything else.

When you're young and there are loads of doctors poking you and prodding you, embarrassment overtakes fear. There were times when it was painful though – having echo scans really used to hurt me. Now when I have scans and ECGs I just laugh because I'm so ticklish.

My mum and dad never made me feel

WHEN YOU'RE YOUNG and there are loads of doctors poking you and prodding you, embarrassment overtakes fear...

like I was any different from anyone else. I just couldn't run as fast as everyone else. I was on beta blockers for a lot of my childhood. Beta blockers are drugs that basically try to help your heart get into a regular rhythm, but the side effects meant I had low blood pressure. I remember collapsing a lot and having seizures. I was very often in and out of hospital.

When I was maybe eleven or twelve years old, I was playing Blousey in *Bugsy Malone*. They let me out of the hospital during the day to rehearse, but I had to go back in overnight. That was strange: it was like being in some sort of hospital prison, because someone was with me all the time, monitoring me. I'd have things hanging off me – monitors and whatever – so I knew I was really ill, but my parents made sure I was never scared or worried about it. They integrated it into daily life, so it felt almost normal. Because of my parents, having heart problems didn't feel like a big deal. It was just normal to me. My friends were great too, they kind of ignored it, which is what you want as a kid. Just to be accepted.

I think I was probably the kind of kid no one would have imagined doing what I do now. I was a sickly, skinny girl who had a slight green tinge to her skin, and who was always in and out of hospital.

There would be times when I'd be acting normal and then I'd just collapse. It was only then that people would realise I wasn't well. I suppose I was good at covering it up and I know I'm very good at that now.

From the ages of around eight to fourteen years old, I would go to King George Hospital in Essex once every few months. I was usually there for tests and monitoring. They'd give me twenty-four tapes and stick an ECG onto my skin. I'd have a little Tamagotchi-like thing that would stick to my belt, and every time I got an irregular heartbeat, I'd press the button so it marked it on the tape. Then they'd look at my actual heartbeat to see if, when I pressed the button, my heart really was irregular. Amazing technology.

Though I was in hospital often, I was always around kids who were way sicker than I was. Luckily, I suppose, I was never in long enough to have to make a life in hospital, to make friends and go to school there.

I was always very shy; I'm still quite shy now. Believe it or not, there are times when I keep myself to myself, and I'm not out there being loud; I love to observe and that's how I was in hospital. I used to like sitting and

IT CAN TAKE A LONG TIME TO WORK OUT WHY, BUT I BELIEVE SOME THINGS HAPPEN FOR A REASON"

doing crosswords, and I'd paint or draw. The way I dealt with spending time in hospital was to write songs, make up poems and draw.

My parents were there every single day. They would talk to me about the weather or football, do the word search with me or generally keep me occupied. In fact, I remember more about how my parents were when I was ill than I do about being ill myself.

At eleven I had to have an ablation, and I was taken to Great Ormond Street Hospital. An ablation is an operation where they put wires in your groin and shoulders and they basically try and buzz your heart into a regular rhythm. I woke up from the anaesthetic and asked, 'Did it work?' and my dad answered, 'No, trust you, you've come all the way here and it didn't work.' It made me laugh, and I think that's one of the reasons why humour, to me, is such a powerful thing. I believe that if you drown in doubt and negativity, it won't help you. Laughter, good energy and positive thinking are much more beneficial.

One of the reasons I'm obsessed with lava lamps to this day is because there was a relaxation room at GOSH, and after my operation I'd go in there and sit and watch the bubbles and lie on mattresses on the floor. I've always wanted a house where I can have a room like that – one day!

While most kids were fine with me, there were, of course, some kids who were horrible. In primary school, the beta blockers literally turned my skin green, that was one of the main side effects. Plus I looked ill: I had sunken eyes and big teeth and a massive fringe. My ponytail was about four strands of hair because my fringe was so big. Sad times. There were a handful of kids that were mean.

Bullying became something I needed to write a song about. 'Who's Laughing Now' was honest: kids really did pull my chair out from under me, they did throw stones at my head. After 'Do It Like A Dude' came out, those people used to Facebook me, asking to hang out. I'd be like, 'Aren't you that person who used to throw stones at me while I was walking home from school?' Just because I've become successful at what I do, it doesn't rewrite the past.

The bullying was never horrific; I've never been beaten up, for instance, but sometimes the words hurt more than the bruises. When you're young, you don't really understand why people behave like that. But I had the most amazing mum and dad and family I could go home to. Not every kid does, which is why I want to make sure they know they're not the only ones going through it. Some of the fan mail I get now is incredible. In some ways I'm almost glad I went through all of that bullying and illness so I could write a song that would one day help people.

It can take a long time to work out why, but I believe some things happen for a reason. But at the end of the day, who is laughing now?

CHAPTER TWO

U S T A N D U P

'If you don't reach for the moon you can't fall on the stars
So I live my life like every day is the last, last, last…'

Stand Up

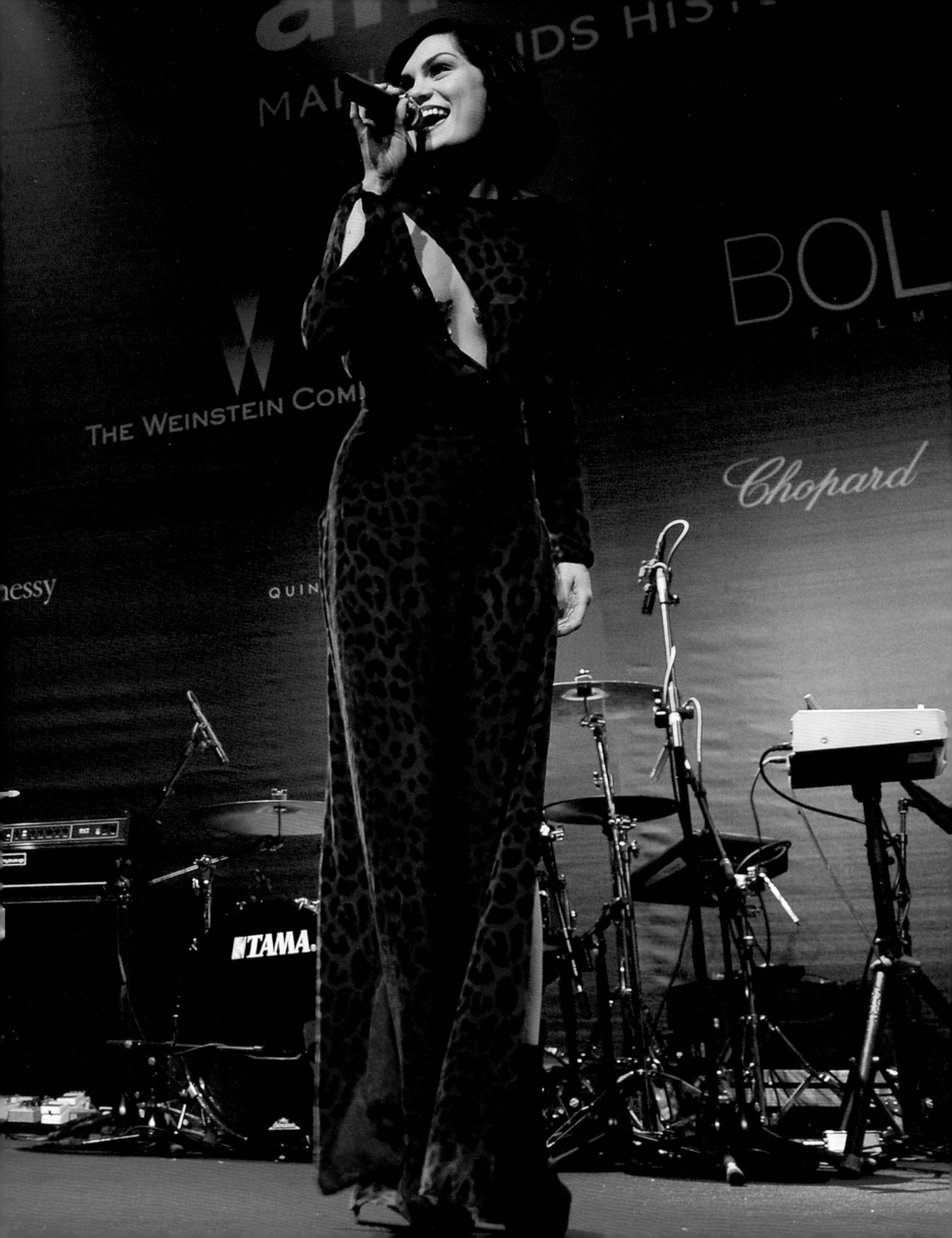
THE WEINSTEIN COM
BOL
Chopard
TAMA

I was ready to grow up and be a big girl for real. Blazer and tie please...

BIG SCHOOL

I went to Mayfield Secondary School. People would have to accept me on my own terms. I felt like, 'I am Jessica Cornish; take it or leave it.' I was always all right with new things and up for a challenge. I was never someone who was scared. I was like, 'Let's have it.' And I was quite good at making new friends. I think. *Waves*.

Mayfield was the school down the road from my old house, so after moving it was a lot of commuting but I didn't want to not be with a majority of my friends from primary school. My sisters went there and they were both head girl. Every day I'd walk in and see their names on a plaque and the teachers would say, 'Oh, you're a Cornish, we have high hopes for you.' So the pressure was on to be well behaved and clever, but I wasn't academic – I'm still not.

Certain things don't soak into my brain. I'm intelligent, but I'm not academic. I'm not someone who can work out massive sums. I remember I got four per cent in my Geography exam, and to this day I struggle to find London on the weather map. *Awkward*.

My GCSE results proved that whatever I liked I got good grades in: I got an A* for Art, an A for Drama, an A for English Lit, a B for English Language, a C for French (*Bonjour, je m'appelle Jessica*) and then three Ds and three Es. My aim was clearly to get every grade across the board! No Fs though, at least I turned up, even if I knew I wasn't going to do very well.

I didn't sing in secondary school, because I didn't feel supported by the school. Which is why I guess I have never been invited back. The music teacher, in my opinion, shouldn't have been teaching. I hope he isn't now. He wasn't a very nice guy. Knowing as much as I do about music, I feel he didn't know what he was talking about. He was just mean.

As a teen, I wasn't allowed to be in the school choir (which he was in charge of). Some of the mums said I stuck out like a sore thumb because I was so loud – not the nicest thing to hear when you're eleven. I remember going home and telling my mum. I was so upset.

I did enjoy secondary school, but if I am honest I kind of wanted to get through it and go and spend every day doing what I really loved.

BRAT
PITT

Let me start this section with a classic clumsy Jess story. As with all stage shows, things do go wrong. One night, I was in the middle of belting out my song 'When Children Rule The World', in my role of Brat in *Whistle Down The Wind* and – in what would become a recurring theme in my career – as I left the stage, I tripped my way into the orchestra pit. I did the most amazing backflip. Sheet music flew into the air and I fell onto the conductor, who amazingly just kept going through sheer shock and disbelief, I think. That's how my musical theatre nickname was created: 'Brat Pitt'. Original.

I don't remember feeling 'special' or different as a kid because I was working on the West End. It wasn't like you'd go every day, because you weren't allowed to as a child. You could do four or five shows a week, and that was it. I got £50 for a matinee and £75 for an evening show. When my mum and dad gave me the money I'd earned from *Whistle* when I was seventeen years old, I gave half of it to them to try and pay back some of the money they'd spent on everything, from costumes to travel. Me

being me, I spent the other half on bongos and random stuff that I didn't really need. I wanted a drum kit but I couldn't afford that, so I got bongos. I still have them. They're... crap.

I auditioned for *Annie* with some friends and I remember all the other girls were really timid and small, and it got to me and I remember being soooo loud. The director was like, 'S***!' I just had a powerful voice and didn't really know how to control it. 'THE SUN WILL COME OUT TOMORROW!'

My other friends got in and I didn't. I walked out and my mum told me, 'When a door slams in your face, it doesn't mean it's the end, it means there is a bigger, more beautiful door waiting for you – you just have to find it.'

About two weeks later, I got a lead role as Brat in Andrew Lloyd Webber's *Whistle Down The Wind* on the West End (I found the door, Mum). While I was in it, my secondary school sang the theme song 'Whistle Down The Wind' for the autumn concert. It's cool. I could see what the music teacher was doing. LOL.

I realised my hobby could become my career after getting the role in *Whistle*.

I hadn't had many singing lessons; I just opened my mouth and sang – loudly by all accounts! I didn't even practise that much. Getting a role in a West End show undoubtedly kick-started everything for me and I wasn't the only one who went on to do well. I was in the original cast and on the original cast recording of *Whistle*, alongside Jade from the Sugababes, James Buckley from *The Inbetweeners* and Bluey Robinson, who is an amazing singer and artist now. I'm sure there are hundreds of others who have become successful – it's a great experience to have when you're young with big dreams.

I went to Colin's Performing Arts in Romford for two years. It was cool. I had moved to Romford by then, so it was a way of attaching myself to the area and getting to know people. Rochelle Wiseman from The Saturdays went there and so did James Buckley. He was hilarious. He used to get in so much trouble at dance school. He was the funniest – even the teachers had to laugh, because he was just so good. Everyone knew he was going to do well. Very proud. Also during that time, I entered something called Britain's Brilliant Prodigies, which was an under-16 competition for kids. I entered the pop singer category. How that isn't online still shocks me. I've still got the DVD – it's hilarious. It's very weird to watch, and I'm just singing while walking around the house. As you do, I said something like, 'I just want people to hear me on the radio and know that it's me.' Weird. I met Sarah Ferguson and Robin Gibb, who presented me with my award

– I was really sad to hear the news that he passed away. He was a legend and a huge part of the history of pop and disco music. He was the first person to say my voice was international. I was so lucky to get to meet him.

"I REALISED MY HOBBY COULD BECOME MY CAREER AFTER THE ROLE IN *WHISTLE*"

Do you know what I love about theatre? People don't shout out. I went to see *Ghost* recently and it struck me how classy theatre is compared to some gigs. I know it's completely different, and there is nothing better than people singing your songs, but some people get so hysterical when they watch a band or singer sometimes; with theatre, you sit and are respectful, just peaceful; you just watch, then cheer at the end. That's one thing that was really hard for me to get used to. It's mad when people are shouting out things like, 'Please can you sign this for me?' while you're singing a ballad. It can be off-putting.

I think now that I like to marry the two. I love people singing along, but I also love the challenge of making people just listen.

BEST OF BRITISH

I auditioned for the The BRIT School in Croydon at sixteen years old, to study musical theatre and fine art for two years. Laura Michelle Kelly, who played my older sister in *Whistle Down The Wind*, recommended it to me. I was so nervous to audition, but when I went and saw it, I fell in love with the freedom of it all. The atmosphere was amazing. I was so happy when I found out I had got in.

I wanted to continue what I had spent my free time doing but make it my everyday focus. It was the only free performing arts school in London so that was a huge bonus, as most of these schools are £10,000 a year, which is just too expensive. I was ready to work hard and learn more about what I loved.

The BRIT School has had many successful artists but, for me, what was most important was all the people who had got into musicals after attending the school. That was my goal then, I was sixteen and just wanted to be on the stage.

The BRIT School is a place to look for opportunity. You can get it if you want it. It was there that I auditioned for the girl group Soul Deep, a band for the Don't Trigger campaign with Mothers Against Guns. In the same week I auditioned for a new MTV programme about a girl who was a runner at a record label and could sing; she gets discovered and then releases songs into the chart as the character, a bit like Hannah Montana.

I kind of feel like the choice I had to make after being lucky enough to be offered both opportunities decided the the path that led me to who I am today. I knew that even though the MTV contract would have been amazing and the money would have helped my mum and dad out, I had to base the decision on what I wanted out of life and what meant something to me.

I sat with my mum and dad and said I wanted to do the Mothers Against Guns campaign, and they said, 'Just follow your heart.'

So very early on, after starting at The BRIT School, I joined Soul Deep, one of three acts to be created specifically for the campaign. Each group recorded a song for the EP; our song was called 'Why' and was very emotional and real. It was a fantastic thing to use my voice for – to educate young people about what guns were doing to our society. I met so many parents who had lost their children. It was so inspiring to see how strong they were, to send out the message that the gun and knife crime in the UK needs to stop. I was honoured that at such a young age I could also help. I really learnt how precious life is.

Around the same time, I was spotted at London Bridge station on my way to The BRIT School to be a hair model for Vidal Sassoon. There are pictures floating around; type 'Metropolis Vidal Sassoon' into YouTube (one you haven't discovered yet?). I had every style

going – from a mohican to a mullet, blue, green, red, you name it. It was weird, because there were buses going down Oxford Street with my big face on them. I might cringe a bit now, but I used that money for singing lessons, so I was grateful for the work and I got to see a lot of the world, even if I had silly hair. I went to Japan, Madrid, Germany. It was an amazing experience, I'm just glad I don't have to do it any more! Bleaching your head HURTS!

For me, my time at The BRIT School was all about gaining confidence, character building and finding out about myself. I saw that singing is acting and acting is singing. It's about being confident when you perform. You do a lot of embarrassing things in musical theatre, so I don't get embarrassed easily. Also, the vocal training I received was incredible. For me, opera and musical theatre are the two best forms of vocal training you can have. It did take me a while to realise, though, that I had to find my 'own' voice. I used to sing in a slightly affected way, as though I was still onstage and needed to project. My natural voice was very different, but I found it pretty much once I started writing my own songs.

When I was at The BRIT School, I had all sorts of friends. I knew Adele; we were in

a really creative, nurturing environment.

When Adele started to take off – Amy Winehouse was already huge by then – it was amazing to have the opportunity to watch and learn. I saw how high Amy and Adele, and many other female UK artists, set the standard. Amy and Adele really pushed boundaries in America. Watching them, it gave me hope that maybe one day it could happen for me too.

One thing about The BRIT School was the distance I had to travel from Romford to Croydon. I took six trains a day, and got up at 5am every day for two years. I had to be dedicated.

At the time I was travelling a long way to get to The BRIT School to do my A-levels, plus I was a hair model, in a girl group and had a job in Hamleys working for Nail Jazz. It was at Hamleys that I started to suffer with pins and needles in my right hand and foot. I ignored it for a few minutes, then realised it was getting worse.

"IT WAS AT HAMLEYS I STARTED TO SUFFER WITH PINS AND NEEDLES"

the same year. We used to hang out at lunchtimes sometimes and have a little jam. The music room was usually the place where everyone would get together and show off, basically. We'd sing songs we'd written or perform whatever we were working on. It was

I phoned my dad, and he told me to go straight to the hospital. I thought I'd be fine, but then I started getting pains in my right leg. I thought I was having a heart attack – a really slow one. I couldn't breathe in.

I don't know how I did it, but I managed to get the train home and went to my local walk-in GP clinic. I'd started having really bad shooting pains in my chest, I couldn't feel my right hand, my mouth wasn't moving much on my right side and my right eye was going blurry. I sat with the doctor and he said, 'I don't want to scare you, but I'm calling an ambulance, because you've had a minor stroke.' I was like, 'F**k, that's dramatic! I thought I had a cold!'

At the hospital, doctors came in and prodded my leg, but I couldn't feel a thing. It was really, really scary. I wasn't a little girl any more, and at eighteen I was a lot more aware of what was happening – very different from when I was young. It's very rare for young people to experience something like that. They say it's caused by an adolescent migraine and stress. I think it was time for me to slow down.

I was in hospital for about two-and-a-half weeks. It meant I had to leave The BRIT School four months early. Thank God I'd worked my arse off before then, because I got three distinctions and didn't need to re-take any of my exams. I didn't want to let myself down, after working so hard.

It took months to recover from my stroke. Once I was up and about, the weight I had gained started to drop off. It just took a while for me to regain my strength and rebuild a lot of muscle loss. I remained positive though, and apart from my right side being achey when I am tired and a trapped nerve I have had under my arm ever since, I'm fine. *Smiles*.

So now when I'm tired I have to rest, I take vitamins and look after myself as much as I can. It's hard to remain well 24/7 and when I do get sick, I will always be letting people down because I have work booked in every day. It's the pressure of knowing you can't be replaced. If my drummer is ill, or my tour manager, someone else can come in for a few shows. If I get sick I can't send in a lookalike.

GUT
FEELING

After leaving The BRIT School at eighteen and recovering, I still recorded with the girl group Soul Deep. We did a showcase in a Caribbean restaurant called Cottons in Camden Town.

It was a huge night for us and to be honest, even though I was excited, I think by this point – after the campaign had ended, and the material we were singing slowly turned into 'I'm in club, look at my body, bla bla bla' – I had kind of lost interest in being in a group and wanted to focus on myself. I had written my first song, 'Big White Room', by this point and knew I had something to say to the world through my songs.

I wanted to do the showcase – I didn't want to let the other members of the group down, and I would also have the opportunity to sing in front of record labels. But I really had no clue about anything back then.

The showcase went well, it was a full house and my manager called me the morning after. I had been offered a solo deal by the independent record label Gut Records.

All the other girls knew I wanted to be a solo artist – I'd been very honest with them since the campaign ended – and they told me to go for it. They were really supportive and understood that it was a moment and a chance I didn't want to let slip away.

I was the first artist to sign to Gut, alongside Crazy Frog – no wonder it didn't work out! *Ring ding ding!* I laugh about it now, but that old saying 'Everything happens for a reason' is definitely in full swing round here. They were a great label though. What was nice about it was I could develop my craft and perform and learn about myself as I was still young. I got to go on tour with Chris Brown, Jools Holland, Cyndi Lauper, the Sugababes and Girls Aloud.

It was an amazing experience doing those tours. I've still got a picture of Cheryl and me from when I supported Girls Aloud. Cheryl came up to me after one of my shows and said, 'You need to be signed; you're amazing. I'm a massive fan.' Ever since then, we've been

Block 22   Row A
Level 2   Seat 17
Possible Hand Rail Obstruction

BRIT AWARDS
with MasterCard 2006

Earls Cour...

...n Entrance – Old Brompton Road
...February 2006
...ow Starts 7.30pm
...Evening Ends 2.00am

...D PARTY

Jessie J.- Gut Records
www.myspace.com/musicjessiej

For information on bookings, PAs, collaborat...
contact 141a Management

If you need producers/ remixers/ writers fo...
projects check out www.141amanagemer...
contact Nadia on +44 (0) 207 582 3...

Gut Recordings
Proudly Presents...

Jessie

www.jessiemusic.co.uk
www.myspace.com/musicjessie

BRIT AWARDS 2006 BALCONY   BALCONY
BALCONY   13APK
Miss J Cornish
YOU WILL NEED THIS TICKET TO BOARD THE COACH
THERE IS NO TOILET ON THE COACH

£ 6.00   Cash

Box Office   314   STANDARD
020 8665 5242   www.brit.croydon.sch.uk

supportive of each other's careers and we always chat when we see each other. It's rare that that happens because we are both very busy, but it's always nice to see someone who believed in you in the really early days.

I've also seen Cyndi Lauper again – we both did *Jools Holland's Annual Hootenanny 2011–12* (I was shouting out, 'Who's your nanny!' – that's quite embarrassing). When we were on tour in 2008, she asked me to join her onstage in Southampton and sing 'Girls Just Wanna Have Fun'. I only knew the chorus and she asked me to sing the second verse. I thought the second verse was the bridge, so I came in on the wrong bit. It was a shambles! But she just went with it like a pro.

While I was signed to Gut, I played all of the big London nights: iluvlive, yOyO and Proud Galleries; they were the main nights that supported up-and-coming artists – they're still around now and they are great places to get to know yourself in front of a true London audience. That was a great creative period for me; I was writing and performing in front of audiences big and small, building my fan base slowly but surely. Personally, I think artists now get signed and pumped out too quickly. They don't get nurtured any more, they don't get looked after, they don't get proper media training. I ended up creating my own fan base online without any help from a label. I think that makes it much more authentic and definitely helped me feel prepared for what lay ahead.

I was with Gut for two years but felt that maybe it wasn't right for me. I remember getting a phone call from my manager at the time. It had something to do with money, and I thought he said something about them going into liquidation. Obviously me and my stupid sense of humour, I said, 'What does that mean, are they going to be soup?'

I didn't know how things were going to work out financially for Gut, but I gathered that I had six weeks to find a new deal or they could end up owning all of my music – everything from the beginning up to that point, including 'Big White Room', 'Technology', 'Catwalk', 'Sexy Silk', 'Stand Up' and 'Mamma Knows Best'.

I'll be honest, there were times when I felt like giving up. I had worked solidly for two years, only for it all to be taken out of my hands. Someone else was in control of my destiny and music; it was a weird time.

I think everyone feels like that at some point. It's whether you've got the stability and the will to carry on. If I'd given up then, who knows what I'd be doing now? I'm all about the energy of feng shui, so I'd probably be feng shui-ing people's lives for them! Either that or maybe doing make-up and styling.

I eventually got signed as a songwriter to Sony/ATV in America. It was a miracle to me because it restored my faith that people still believed in me. A lot of the songs, apart from the ones I kept for myself, were given to other people: Chris Brown had 'I Need This' for his *Graffiti* album and I placed 'Owe It All To You' and 'Smoke' on *Smoke*, the album of Lisa Lois (the winner of Holland's *X Factor*). 'Sexy Silk' was going to be my first single – it was on a Nivea advert and it was later named the biggest selling song on the *Easy A* soundtrack.

The next step was to try to get re-signed as a solo female singer in the UK. That's when the challenge began, as all the UK labels had too many girls to start fresh on a new one and invest in a project that was in very early stages – you had Adele, Ellie Goulding, Amy Winehouse, Little Boots and Cheryl all releasing, and lots more.

I was a little sad, but again I knew it was more about business than me. It's crazy what you learn through knock-backs. I was realising I had to believe in myself more than anyone else.

I flew to the US to do some writing and clear my head, and work out what I was going to do next. Sony/ATV hooked me up with some writers and made sure I was busy when I was there. If I couldn't make it happen in the UK, well, I'd just have to fly across the Atlantic and make it happen over there. It wasn't about running away, it was about making it work. I wasn't giving up.

We did two showcases while I was in America: one was in New York at SOB's and the other in LA at The Viper Room. I had no idea it was any kind of big deal, and rolled up and performed like it was a normal show. But that was when everybody came down: every major record label had heard it was on and came down to check me out. It was rammed – just shows you. (Mum, I found another door.)

I was gobsmacked when days later I was in discussion with six major labels. Bosses were phoning the UK labels saying, 'What were you thinking letting this one go?'

I had a huge decision to make, and even though I was experienced in performing, I wasn't so experienced when it came to major labels and business, and how hardcore they all get. I decided Universal Republic felt like the right record label for me. I wanted to go with Universal because I really liked the way they involved everyone in the showcase. It wasn't just the big bosses, it was every single person there (I'm a sucker for a family vibe), and the artists they looked after were ones I like. Monte Lipman and Jason Flom, the CEOs of the record label, understood what my dreams were and wanted to help me make them a reality.

I also wanted to sign with Universal Island in the UK, and their deal would give me that option. The thing I like about them is the way they let their artists have some creative control. I wanted to sign with Island partly because of their incredible history with Bob Marley, U2 and Amy Winehouse, and partly because of their president, Darcus Beese; he was A&R when I tried to get signed the first time and was then promoted to CEO of the record label. When I'd tried to get signed before, I'd really liked Darcus. I knew he could help take me where I wanted to be. So I signed with him in the UK as part of my deal because he's just... well... cool. He gets me as a person. I'll be honest, Gut not working out was a blessing in disguise as, even though I had moments of doubt, I had been given the best opportunity to be represented by Universal worldwide. BOOM!

PARTY IN THE USA

I've actually never met Miley Cyrus, still... to this day... which is jokes.

One of my first sessions after being signed with Universal was while I was in America, with Dr. Luke and Claude Kelly. People told me that Luke was scary. In fact I just took the piss about the fact that he had a mouse on his pink T-shirt, and he took the piss about how much blusher I was wearing – match made in heaven! They'd both already had some big hits, so I was really excited to be working with them. I remember being in the studio, trying to find another single. That's one thing you should know: you're always trying to find another single!

Anyway, I remember we wrote 'Party In The USA' during that first session. Dr. Luke played me the guitar lick. I wanted to write a song about being a UK chick going to the US and being a bit nervous about it. I jammed out with Claude (one of my closest friends and one of the nicest guys I have met in the industry) and Luke, and the song came together very naturally. We loved it and the label loved it, but everyone felt it wasn't edgy enough for me – it felt a bit young. Luke said that Miley was looking for a track, so he sent it to Disney and within three weeks she'd recorded it. Miley actually asked permission to use some of the ad libs, the vocal flourishes that I'd improvised, which was really nice.

I remember Luke texting me, telling me that 'Party In The USA' had gone to number one on iTunes. I don't think I realised how big a deal that was. I didn't believe him, so he sent me a picture of the iTunes chart, showing Miley at number one. I was like, 'I don't really know what this means, but I know it's good, especially in America.' As I said before, I was still learning. I then told everyone I knew within in ten minutes (I don't know many people).

Co-writing that song did so much for me. I've always said this: I much prefer to be known for writing a quadruple-platinum song that was number one in eight countries than for featuring on a song with a rapper, which was what everyone was doing at the time. I wanted to do something different and a bit more credible. That's why I was glad I was given that opportunity and it definitely opened the door to America for me. I was a nobody but people were so interested in that song, they really started to look at me as a songwriter. It was a risk, but that's what I'm about: taking risks. And I've always said a winner is a winner before they win.

Me at The BRITs, 2012.

CHAPTER THREE

DOING IT LIKE A DUDE

'Stomp, stomp, I've arrived...'

Do It Like A Dude

All of those years of singing and writing and waiting were about to pay off.

What I didn't know is that this would be the toughest test of all...

YOUTUBE
SENSATION

It was out of frustration that I put up my first YouTube video. I remember being like, I'm just doing it. I'd been signed for two, three years and I was ready to put out an album. I just wanted people to hear my music. Gut had told me it was hard to get people interested in me because no one knew me. I responded, 'OK, well then, I'll find a way to get people talking about me.' *Diva finger snap, hair flick*. I didn't do that. LOL.

I started thinking about what I could do and where I could put my music out that would get it directly to the fans and the people, instead of going through management and a label. I realised that the Internet was the best way to go. It's funny thinking about it now, because it became such a big part of my career, but back then the idea of me doing YouTube videos wasn't supported by everyone around me.

They thought no one would be interested in hearing original music by someone they'd never heard of, but to me that was the whole point. I didn't want to do

covers; that's what everyone else was doing. I wanted people to hear me doing my own music. At the beginning at least. Let people really base their opinion on me and what I did.

'Mamma Knows Best', 'Stand Up' and 'Big White Room' were the first three tracks I put up. 'Mamma Knows Best' and 'Stand Up' I put up when I was in the UK, and 'Big White Room' while I was in LA. I remember sitting on my bed and deciding there and then to do a video. I went into the bathroom and sang 'Big White Room' in one take. I had no clue how to edit, so it was one take or nothing. If you have seen the video, that's why I couldn't take the elbow knock out. It showed how clumsy and uncool I was though. Haha!

I put it online and then watched the numbers start to rise and rise – it was as simple as that. Almost immediately people would stop me in the shops and say, 'You're that girl from YouTube.' I saw that it worked, so I went with what worked. It was really that simple.

From 100 people watching, it grew to thousands, to hundreds of thousands – and this was in 2009, nearly two years before I released 'Do It Like A Dude'. You can tell a lot of people who put out videos have spent hours doing their hair and make-up and thinking about what they're going to wear and where they've set up. In my videos, there are no sheets on the bed, there's a hoover in the background, there's also deodorant – and I'm in my pyjamas, singing. To this day people still say, 'Why do you have a hoover in your bedroom?' My answer is still, 'Why not?' I had been hoovering.

There were no gimmicks and I think that's what people liked. It was just about my voice. I wasn't trying to be anything more than a girl who was sitting on her bedroom floor in her pyjamas, singing a song.

I found YouTube and YouTube found me. Forever grateful.

TRUTH OR DARE

Thanks to the YouTube videos, people had heard me sing, but they had very little idea about who I was as a person. I wanted people to get to know me. I was now signed to a label in the UK and in America, and working hard to make sure I was being portrayed as myself, musically and personality-wise. We were preparing for 'Do It Like A Dude' and 'Price Tag' to come out and I had built that online presence. Now I wanted people to get to know me as a person. As I think people probably know now, I can be very serious, but I can also be really silly and childish!

As much as I love doing what I do, it can get so busy that I forget to have fun. When I signed to Universal, it started to get to the point where everything was serious, and it was all meetings and contracts and decisions. There were management meetings, label meetings, styling meetings, meetings about meetings...! It seemed like I had to be ten years older than I was at the time; I had to be very grown up. I was craving some mischief.

So I decided to create something that meant I could have fun but also included my fans; an online programme, *Dare Jessie J*.

It was an eight-part series where I asked fans and celebrities like Perez Hilton, B.o.B and N-Dubz to dare me to do stupid things. It was brilliant! I could go and dress up as Rudolph in Carnaby Street and sing 'Twinkle, Twinkle, Little Star' and go on roller coasters. I love making people laugh and not taking myself too seriously.

I haven't done a *Dare Jessie J* for a while now, but I do still make silly videos to say 'Hi'. I do them very specifically now. I don't like to do them for the sake of it, I prefer to do them when there's a valid reason; getting a number one, selling out a tour or just as a little treat for myself and my fans. They get me a little emotional, because they remind me of where I started. I did one this year when I was in Thailand with all my friends and I went to number one with 'Domino'. I had all of my friends doing the chorus; it was just us being silly and messing about, but people enjoy them, that's what counts.

A defining moment in my career has to be my first *Later... with Jools Holland* performance. In the industry, getting to perform on *Jools* as a new artist is a really, really big deal. I did the show in November 2010. It was Tinie Tempah's first performance on the show too; he was doing 'Pass Out' and I was performing 'Price Tag'. It was one of the first times we met, and we've become good friends since. It's so nice to have someone who understands the crazy things you experience in the rise to success.

At that point, I was very aware of what I wanted to do as a female pop, R&B and soul singer. I wanted to cross over, to be able to do Coachella, Glastonbury and *Jools* and perform at venues like KOKO in Camden. I wanted to do everything; I wanted to be urban, I wanted to be pop, but I wanted to be musically left-field as well. My goal was to encompass all of my influences, put my own spin on them and create something commercial but credible.

Being on *Jools* and being allowed to do an acoustic performance was so important to me. The same day, the 'Do It Like A Dude' video dropped. It was very aggressive and dramatic: spiky lips, bomber jacket, crotch-grabbing. On *Jools*, I was just in jeans and a T-shirt.

I'll be honest, as I waited for the camera to spin round to me, my heart was beating so hard I could feel it in my throat. The show being live is scary enough but all I could think was that my granddad could watch it and so could a 15-year-old girl in Doncaster. Jools Holland appeals to so many audiences, a performance on *Jools* can quite literally make or break you. All I could think was: 'This is it now. Don't sneeze.' LOL.

All of those years of preparation and praying and wishing that I could be out there and have people hear my music... And as soon as it goes – if it goes – it really goes. There's no switching it off. It's gone. You've gone. And that's what happened.

From then on, every day began with getting up at 6am and ended after returning home around midnight. Everything happens so fast, you barely get time to take it all in. It was great, it was amazing, but it's the hardest year, I think, of anyone's career because you are so not prepared for it. You just have to take a deep breath and do it and enjoy every second. My dreams were coming true.

GO GO GO

In 2011, I went through three passports. Three. All with equally as dodgy pictures. That should give a rough idea of how far and wide I travelled throughout the year. Crazy! From Scotland to Sydney, Kuala Lumpur to Los Angeles, I had no idea how far music could – and would – take me, literally. It's a global language for sure. As 2010 went on, I could feel the pace picking up. I'd had the Miley success, I'd signed my deal with Universal in the US and the UK, I was on top of the world and I'd written most of my debut album. I'd seen my fans grow from basically my mum and dad to millions on YouTube. Magazines started requesting interviews, the live shows started to get a little bit bigger, I was being recognised in the street and there was talk of BRITs nominations and a performance on *Later... with Jools Holland*. I was cautiously optimistic. I was still learning to trust and let go despite past experiences.

I'd been close to this before and I knew how the music industry worked. It takes years to get it and moments for it all to be taken away. I wanted to make sure we got it exactly right; I had no idea, of course, just how right (and occasionally not so right) it would all go. All part of the journey.

Whatever happened, I was ready to show the world that I could sing. That's the only thing I'm ever focused on, singing. I don't care about anything else. If I'm backstage before a gig or a TV show and my hair isn't done, I'm still going out. I'm not missing my set. If I have a performance or an appearance, I'll go out in a black bag, my fingernails not painted, my eyelashes hanging off. I don't give a s***. (I did once have a wardrobe meltdown in Australia, but it was a

> ## "AS LONG AS I SING WELL, THAT'S ALL THAT MATTERS"

one-off! I'll tell you about that later.) As long as I sing well, that's all that matters.

I had no idea at that point, but I was about to embark on the busiest, craziest, strangest, most exciting, extraordinary, hardest twelve months of my life.

WINNING

Winning the Critics' Choice BRIT and the BBC Sound of 2011, and being nominated for the MTV Brand New for 2011, I was so happy. I finally felt like I was accepted as an artist. Winning two out of the three was just overwhelming. There were some incredible artists nominated alongside me and it was such an honour for a new artist like me to receive those accolades, not just from fans

> ## I KNOW NOT EVERYONE HAS A CHANCE TO MAKE THEIR DREAMS A REALITY"

but from the music industry as well – all the people who had watched me grow and work hard were supporting me. It felt amazing.

Winning the Critics' Choice really sunk in properly at the BRITs launch. When I was a kid, I'd watch The BRITs, and say, 'Mummy, I wanna be her, I wanna sing on the stage' and she'd say, 'You will one day.' I know not everyone has a chance to make their dreams a reality, so I don't take it for granted for one second. I was one of those little kids who would watch all those people going up and collecting awards.

I remember going to The BRITS with The BRIT School and watching Kanye and Dizzie and wishing I was at the event too. So it's very weird when you go from being someone in the audience to someone the audience is watching.

It's overwhelming to win all of those awards; you never think you're going to win, you never expect it. Even more than that, there were some brilliant artists in both of those categories that year: James Blake and Clare Maguire, not to mention Adele, Florence + The Machine and Ellie Goulding, who were past winners. I felt incredibly privileged.

THE BRITS

I remember how nervous I was even though I knew I had won the award prior to the BRITs taking place. I was so nervous. I got up at around 6am and just paced around my flat, practising in my shoes! I was making sure I had everything ready, but I didn't prepare a speech. I was told to prepare one so that I wouldn't waffle, as everyone knows I love a waffle. But I just wanted to speak from the heart.

I remember one of my best friends saying to me, 'Jess, just enjoy it.' I took a deep breath and, once I'd done that, I relaxed and enjoyed myself. I was asked to perform at The BRITS Party, which was like a wedding but with lots of music people. I don't know if anyone was getting married. LOL. There were smoke machines, which went off while I was in the middle of performing 'Dude', and I remember literally jumping when they did as I had completely forgotten about them.

I got to meet Rihanna for the first time at The BRITS, and we spoke about swapping dresses. She was like, 'I want your dress', and I was like, 'I don't think I'd look as good in yours, but I'm happy to swap if you want!' She was very cool and so beautiful.

You know what was nice about winning? I remember being at Alton Towers when Adele won the Critics' Choice Award in 2008. I remember wanting so much to be there, for that to be me, and then, three years later, it all became real. The show started and it hit me: 'F**k, I'm at The BRITS and I am raising a glass tonight!'

When they called me up on stage to accept it, I remember thinking, 'Just don't fall in these shoes.' They were Christian Louboutins – the highest shoes ever. I remember taking them off later that night and having to walk around on tip toe for a bit because I couldn't relax my feet. I had them on for, like, nineteen hours.

As I walked up onto the stage and saw my Snow White (Ellie G, that's what I call her), it all hit me. I started shaking and I just realised I had achieved something really high on my wish list. I wanted to thank everyone who had helped and supported me in getting there. It was so emotional. That's why I got tearful when I accepted the award; I'd worked so hard to get to that spot.

Before I knew it, it was over and time to go to the after-parties – I call them 'afters' because they're not really parties, they're so dry! I probably shouldn't say that. Oh well, quote me ;)

Actually, 2012's BRITs after-party was good because Will.i.am was there, as were Cover Drive, and I was hanging with them and Tinie and Tinchy Stryder. It's nice because I know them now, but no one really knew me back in 2011.

I think people couldn't work me out because of 'Do It Like A Dude'; they didn't know if I was approachable. As I said, I am quite shy in crowds of people and I'm quite shy when it comes to talking to other artists, because I don't want to come across like I'm beggin' it. I'm not someone who has hundreds of friends in the industry. I'm very particular about who I have in my life now, because back then some people who were in my life were not good for me. At the end of the day, just because we sing, it doesn't mean we're going to get on. That's not realistic. It's like anything else: all the teachers at a primary school don't become best friends just because they work at the same school and they like teaching kids.

I enjoyed it a lot more the second time around, at The BRITs in 2012, once I knew a few more people and people knew me, so at the 2012 after-parties I had some serious fun.

One thing that was said early on is that I don't drink, but I do drink now and then. I remember how this whole teetotal thing started. I was in Germany, and I'd just gone to number one with 'Price Tag'. One of the journalists asked, 'How are you going to celebrate? Are you gonna get smashed? Take some drugs?' I said, 'I'm not a big drinker but I'll probably go out and party.' And that was it: 'Jessie J doesn't drink!' I never said that; I'd said I didn't get smashed up, crazy drunk every day. I don't have time to. If I did, I would be hungover every day, and I would never be able to have the career that I do if I was hungover. Nothing is easy when you are hungover.

When it comes to drinking alcohol, firstly, it depends on who I'm with. I've got to be around people I trust. Secondly, even now if I'm seen with a glass of wine, I get slated. People will tweet me and say, 'But you said you don't drink.' I've always been clear: I'm not an alcoholic, I don't use alcohol to become myself, I don't drink every day and I don't do drugs. But if I want to go out and get tipsy, I'm allowed. I'm twenty-four years old, I should be allowed to go and have a drink now and then. Obviously, with my heart, I have to be careful but I know my limits. I respect them.

When I let go, my friends think I'm hilarious; I've got no inhibitions. It's funny, and it's when I make the most mistakes. I get very giggly and flirtatious and sexual when I'm drunk, but I like to have a good time and I love to dance.

Do you know when I was drunk? The 2012 BRITs after-party. I remember saying to my friends in the bathroom, 'I'm so drunk, how am I going to disguise this?' They rightly said, 'Jess, you're allowed to have a drink, you don't have to hide it.' They are right, I have to live my life for me and make sure I am not always thinking about what everyone else will say. It was my version of drunk – three glasses of champagne and a bit giddy – but there were so many paps around. If you've seen the picture of me bending over sticking my bum out, wearing yellow, it was that night and I was trying to disguise that I was drunk. My friends were laughing at me the whole way home.

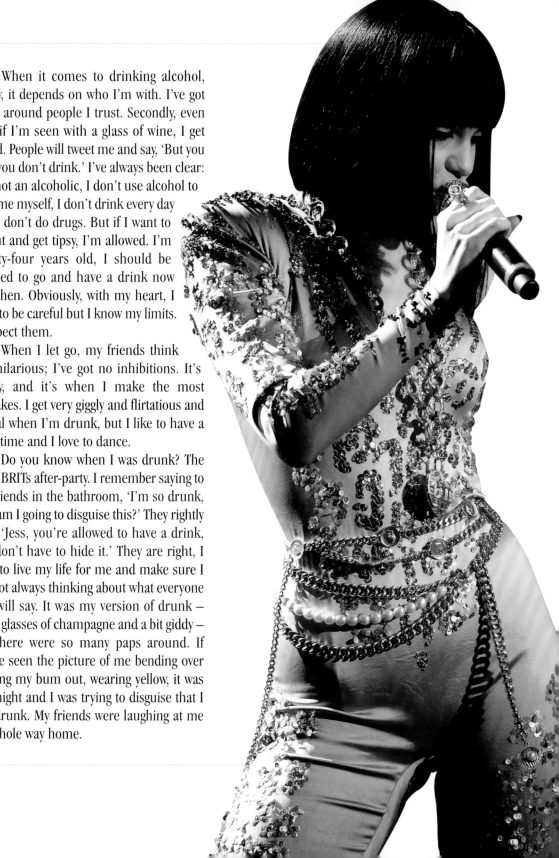

CHAPTER FOUR TRACK BY TRACK

'Just be true to who you are…'

Who You Are

It's often said that you have your whole life
to make your first album; in my case, that's certainly true.
Beginning with the idea for 'Big White Room' at eleven
years old to writing it when I was seventeen, *Who You Are*
really is a lyrical journey through the first twenty-two
years of my life.

As a thank you to the fans, we released a platinum version
in November 2011 and added three more tracks. 'Domino'
gave me a UK number one and a US number six, while
'LaserLight' made history: I was the first British female
artist to have six top-ten hits from one album. *Who You Are*
means so much to me because, in addition to
over 15 million combined sales and an amazing array
of awards and accolades, it's also an incredibly personal
album, and I'm very, very proud of it.

MY FIRST ALBUM

Who You Are **is definitely a reflection of** me growing up. It's the doubts, the beauty, the pain, the belief, the fear and the happiness all put into melodies. You get a real insight into my thought process was when I was a teenager growing into a young woman, and how I put that into my music as honestly as I could.

One thing I wanted to ensure was that people would feel like they could take over the world too. Injecting hope was what I was about in my life after all the knock-backs so, naturally, that's the message my debut album carried. It was just simply: be who you are.

It was recorded in London, LA and NY. I'm so thankful that I got to work with producers and songwriters of such different styles and genres – they all catered to my eclectic taste in music and writing. I didn't want my album to be fourteen songs that

sounded the same. So working with lots of different people, from Dr. Luke to Toby Gad, from The Invisible Men to Oak – it was crucial to making it work for my sound.

I wanted my music to be therapy, as that is what music is to me – a creative outlet. I didn't want it to come and go, to be hot in the club one minute and gone the next. I am a fan of albums that stand the test of time, that have the power of longevity, so that's what I wanted to achieve.

I've always said that if Michael Jackson hadn't put on that white glove, he wouldn't be quite the legend he is now. You have to learn what makes you tick and what's right for you at the right time. I saw a big gap in the market for someone to sing about real life and to be honest and open about having flaws and not being perfect. That's how you feel when you're a teenager, we're all just

"
I'VE ALWAYS SAID
that if Michael Jackson hadn't put on that white glove, he wouldn't be quite the legend he is now
"

finding our way through life and trying to be accepted. So that's what I wanted to write about, because it was what I was going through.

People ask how I write songs. I don't know how, it just happens. If you start thinking about it too much, it often doesn't work. I think if you psyche yourself out and over-think it, that's when you end up with writer's block. I make sure I'm not precious in any sense; I can write to beat and I can write to a guitar. I can arrive with song lyrics, or I can start fresh when it just has to come from the heart. I think you have to be able to adapt, because that's what life is about. You can't go around expecting everyone to mould to what you do. I'm not about to start saying, 'I can only make music if you sit there and the lights are off and there are fourteen candles burning.'

There's one thing I do think about when I go into the studio, and it's something my dad told me. He said, 'Open yourself up when you're in there, but make sure you close yourself back down before you return to the real world.' I think he's right. You expose so much of yourself in the studio, often to strangers, that when you finish you have to make sure you leave those emotions in the studio.

Lauryn Hill's album *The Miseducation of Lauryn Hill* really got me to start writing songs. From there, my family and my friends and my own life inspired what I would write about. I don't listen to other people's songs and try to do 'my version'. I just keep my life

interesting so I have plenty to write about! Aries adventures :)

I love listening to old-school music for inspiration – how they would harmonise back in the day fascinates me. Growing up, the artist I aspired to be was a genius like Beyoncé, with the longevity of someone like Prince – someone who, when you see them twenty, thirty years into their career, is still killing it.

The album *Who You Are* was for me like a musical theatre show, because every song was so different. I'm glad I got to showcase my voice in different ways – from 'Dude' to 'Rainbow' to 'Casualty Of Love' – and to be the different characters that I am in my life.

I would have re-vocalled everything in the same week because it just sounded so detached. People come and see me live and they're surprised by how different I sound. That's because some of that album was recorded nearly seven years ago, and some, like 'Domino', more recently. It's crazy to think every song from *Who You Are* was on YouTube before the album was even released. It was my way to convince the non-believers that such a broad-in-sound album would work.

I have grown up so much since *Who You Are*; music is a continuation of moments and albums are a collection of those moments that we experience in one place. So the collection of moments on the second album will be different from *Who You Are,* as I am a woman now. The journey continues.

TRACK BY TRACK

Here's a rundown of each of the sixteen tracks from **Who You Are,** *released 28 February 2011*

PRICE TAG
Released 30 January 2011

I co-wrote 'Price Tag' in 2009 with Claude Kelly (Moon Head!) and Dr. Luke (Coconut Man!) (I was Pea). It's funny, because I got an email from lawyers at Universal asking me to explain our nicknames because they thought they were racial. That's what people do; it's mad. Luke is Coconut Man because he drinks coconuts all day – like, five a day, straight out of the actual coconut. Claude's got a massive head, so I call him Moonhead, and I've got a tiny head, so I'm Pea. That's it. It's that simple.

'Price Tag' is who I am as an artist. I wanted to write a song about how the industry is based on percentages and sales and wearing sunglasses indoors. *Is it hot where you are?*

Having B.o.B feature on the original and Devlin on the remix was amazing, because I think they both add something extra-special. I'm a huge fan of Devlin, he supported me on my Heartbeat tour in 2011. Not only is he a talented rhymer but, as he's also from Essex, he's one of the coolest, most real people you'll meet.

I asked B.o.B to feature on 'Price Tag' because I really liked his music. His lyrics, his videos – everything about him hit me.

I made four plane journeys in four days: we flew to New York City for a day, then to Buffalo, then to Chicago, then we flew back to London – just to get his bars on it. Dedication. But I wanted to make sure we did it together. He's the only feature artist on the album so I wanted to be involved and actually make music together rather than send parts over email. He rocked into the studio with a guitar on his back and we got into it.

Promoting 'Price Tag' was the hardest thing I've ever done in my life. I have sung that song A LOT. We did three months' promotion in America, taking two plane journeys a day. We were going from Florida to Hawaii to New York to Texas – everywhere. I've got footage on my laptop that no one's ever seen: I'm asleep. Every time you see me in a car, I'm asleep. I took naps all the time because I didn't get to sleep properly. It was crazy.

I think, on average, I was singing 'Price Tag' four times a day. I'm so happy it was that song, because it's the easiest song to sing but I love telling the story of it. Boy, if that had been 'Nobody's Perfect' or 'Who You Are' or 'LaserLight', that would have been tough! 'LaserLight' is SO HIGH! Haha!

"I REMEMBER TELLING THE WAITRESS THAT I WAS NUMBER ONE"

When 'Price Tag' went to number one, I was in Stoke-on-Trent. It was really, really quiet in the town and the restaurant we were in was totally empty. I was there with my guitarist, my radio plugger and my tour manager. I remember telling the waitress that I was number one and she just kind of looked at me and said, 'What do you want to drink?' It was so random. I was really excited but there was no one around, it was raining,

I was in the middle of nowhere and I was eating a margherita pizza. It was so funny.

NOBODY'S PERFECT
Released 30 May 2011

This song is among my favourites on the album. It's one of the most honest songs I've written, about how I chatted behind someone's back once and the person I said things to told the person I was talking about. It spiralled out of control. It's good to vent but you have to trust the people you're venting to. I learned my lesson there: karma really does get you.

I went into the studio the next day with Claude and said I wanted to write a song about it. I wanted it to be straight to the point, raw and full of regret. It was my apology song. Every time I sing it, I relive the moment when I wrote it. I think it's important to expose your flaws in music as well as your strengths. As it says, nobody's perfect, and I'm definitely not!

ABRACADABRA

Luke, Claude and I wrote this song during the same few days that we wrote 'Price Tag'. I was in the studio in LA for about a week with them, toying with ideas and trying to come up with singles and strong album tracks. Luke was playing all of these big beats and I said I fancied doing something a bit more throwback, a bit more old-school. So we listened to some early Mary J. Blige, Mariah Carey and Whitney Houston. I wanted something a bit *Dreamgirls*, some razzle-dazzle R&B. It was one of the few songs on the album that hadn't gone online before the album was released, so I was excited for people to hear it for the first time.

BIG WHITE ROOM

Ben Martinez is playing guitar on the recording of this version of 'Big White Room'.

I wrote it in my mum and dad's house, the house where I was born. The beat was so simple, I was instantly drawn to it; it sounded like *The Lion King*! If I listen to it now, the lyrics are quite childish and there's no structure, but that's as it should be, because I was seventeen years old when I wrote it. Now it's one of the most important tracks to me; it's like my comfort blanket.

The song is about when I was eleven years old and in Great Ormond Street Hospital, opposite a boy who was also about ten or eleven. I remember waking up in the night and hearing him pray because he was having a heart transplant the next day. It was the first time I'd really seen prayer or religion so close up and actually seen someone asking for his life to be saved. He was on his knees, with all these wires hanging out of him, praying. He passed away the next day. I remember asking my mum why God didn't save him. It stuck with me, and it's still there, every day. Every time I sing the song, in my head I dedicate it to that boy and to anyone who's going through the serious, hard, emotional stuff that we have to deal with in life.

It's the only song on the album that was recorded live. We tried and tried to record it with different producers, but it never felt right. We recorded the album version at my first Scala show in London: it was just my guitarist and me, and it came out perfectly. It's one of two songs that I see as connecting all of the others, bringing together all the songs that I've written on my journey so far. It has now had over 8,000 YouTube covers across the world, from Japan to New York to Paris. It's pretty incredible to think it was the first song I wrote at home and now it's become a song that is known across the world. I'm very proud of that track. It's where it all began.

CASUALTY OF LOVE

The label didn't want this on the album – not at all. I had to fight so hard to change their mind because they just weren't into it. I was a bit naughty because I put it on YouTube, and it got an incredible reaction from the fans. So I took that to the label and said, 'Look!' I'm really glad it's on there because the album wouldn't be the same without it. It was, again, inspired by the R&B music I loved when I was growing up. It's about fighting for love. Love on love's terms. This is such a beautiful song, it flows so well and it's one of the most emotional tracks on the album.

RAINBOW

I wrote this song years ago. It's about the world needing to pull together, whether you have money or you're on the dole, whether you're a student or a business person, whether you're black, white or Chinese. We're all different but we all bleed red. It's uniting music – the music I've always wanted to make. I loved recording this song; it was one of the first songs where I had the confidence to adopt characters and adapt my vocal. Even now, when I listen to it, I turn up the volume to level ten and sing along at full blast. 'We're the colours of the rainbow YEAAAAHHHH!'

WHO'S LAUGHING NOW
Released 4 September 2011

This song is for those people who didn't believe in me, the teachers who told me off in class, the teacher who didn't allow me to be in the choir, the people who teased me as a kid but want to be friends now. It was me putting my middle finger up and the only song of its kind on the album. I'm not an arrogant or cocky person, but I needed this one song on there not only to acknowledge the people who have supported me but also to thank the non-believers who tried to hold me back and failed.

DO IT
LIKE A DUDE
Released 22 November 2010

I wrote 'Do It Like A Dude' for Rihanna. At the time Tinie's 'Pass Out' was big and 'Rude Boy' was too, and I wanted to write something in a similar vein. If you listen to the original demo, you can hear me trying to sing it like Rihanna.

My label and I had this inside joke about the first single, and so before I pitched the song to Rihanna and Roc Nation I sent an email to Monte and Jason saying, 'How about this for my first single? Haha.' The people and the powers that be said, 'This is your first single', and that was that. I was like, you know what, it's fun and it's edgy. Let's do it!

The song shows a side of my personality that does exist, but mostly in my personal life, like when I'm out clubbing with my friends. It has more of a humorous but slight rebellious and sarcastic element, which you don't see as much of on the album *Who You Are*. When I wrote it with The Invisible Men, I wanted to create a song that girls ran out of the toilets to dance to. It was fun, it was totally taking the mick; it wasn't serious.

There are a lot of egos and there's a lot of testosterone in the music industry, and I thought it was about time that someone wrote a girls' anthem to show we can be as bad-ass as the boys. *Throws bad-ass pose*.

I wanted to drop 'Dude' and then switch it round and show people a different side of me in 'Price Tag'.

'Do It Like A Dude' doesn't have any secret, hidden messages; it is what it is. I knew people were going be offended by it; I knew some people were going to love it and others were going to hate it. That's what I love about my music. I want to be Marmite; I don't want to be lukewarm water. I want people to love it or hate it. I don't want people to shrug and say, 'She's OK.'

After the song came out digitally in November, there were a lot of people doing remixes, putting their take on it. They all had a sexual connotation, but I don't actually talk about sex once in my version.

It was meant to be fun; it was me parodying myself. I still love performing it. It's a track that everyone can get involved in! 'Stomp, stomp, I've arrived' was the perfect lyric to begin my journey. I wanted people to know I had arrived.

I remember hearing 'Do It Like A Dude' in the back of a cab on the radio for the first time. I was going to a friend's birthday and it came on, and I screamed and then filmed me and my friends miming to it. I wound down the window to see if anyone else was nodding their heads to it. I was on cloud nine!

MAMMA
KNOWS BEST

This song has been with me for years; it was one of the first that I put online and it got a lot of love from people on YouTube. It really helped my career; it got people listening to

me and talking about me. I'm happy it's on the album, but I sing better when the adrenaline is pumping – nerves make me sing better – so 'Mamma' will never be as good recorded as it is live. I want to bring more of 'Jessie J onstage' to the second album. I want to be able to get across better on record how I am live next time. It'll be a challenge, but I'm always up for a challenge.

L.O.V.E.

It's a very special story, this one. I didn't intend the label or anyone else to hear it. It's such a personal song and I knew people would want to ask me about it, then, of course. It was sent to Christina Aguilera and Alicia Keys, but neither of them ended up using it, so when it kept coming back to me I saw it as a sign. I tried hard not to put in on the album, but I loved it so much, I couldn't help it. I love it when the crowd sing along.

STAND UP

This is one of the most important songs to me; I live by every one of the lyrics on this song – I even got the title tattooed on my wrist on New Year's Eve, 2009. With all that I'd been through with my health, I know that life isn't guaranteed; you have to go for it and believe in yourself. You will make mistakes and offend people, contradict yourself, wear terrible outfits, mime when you've always said you'd only sing live, wear shoes you said you'd never wear. It's a song I wrote a long time ago but the words still have the same meaning they did when I wrote it them.

I NEED THIS

I decided to put this on my album because I thought it would be cool to show my version of a song that had already been used by Chris Brown on his *Graffiti* album. I wrote it about my life going from normal to not so normal, and how I needed my friends and family to understand that I needed space to grow. I thought it would be good for people to hear how a song changes when you give it to someone else to adapt, so this is my version. I've always loved it, and it's a great one to sing live.

WHO YOU ARE
Released 7 November 2011

I'd been in LA for three months and was feeling lost, down and missing my family. I didn't know who I was any more. I looked in the mirror and had a talk to myself, and the words just came out: 'Don't lose who you are in the blur of the stars.' I've got that line tattooed on me and in typical Jessie fashion it's spelled wrong – 'Don't loose' instead of 'lose' – but, hey, nobody's perfect! I started to write the song in my head and the next day I went to the studio. I felt so upset, I cried the whole day; at that point I didn't know if I wanted to give up on the industry altogether. Never the music, just the industry.

On the flight home the next day, I listened to it and felt like I'd saved myself in some way. Sometimes you write songs for other people, but other times you write music for yourself. Like 'Big White Room', 'Who You Are' was the perfect song to link all of the others together; it sums up everything I've been through. Sometimes you don't get the chance to stop and think about what – and who – is important to you. You really do have to remember who you are; that's why I wanted it to be my album title

DOMINO
Released 20 February 2012

When I wrote 'Domino' I didn't feel sexy and free, I had broken my ankle. So I wanted to write a song that made me feel sexy and free, and it does every time I sing it.

MY SHADOW

I wrote this song about someone in my family who was very close to me. I was in the studio, not long after they had passed away, and realised that people don't write songs for funerals any more. I know that's a weird thing to think, but if someone died now, what would you want to play from the radio today? 'Earthquake'? 'Do It Like A Dude'? There's nothing like 'Wind Beneath My Wings' or 'I Will Always Love You' any more. I wanted to write a song to offer support to people who have just lost someone. I know I'm going to need that song myself one day. I meet a lot of kids who have lost friends and family members, and I wanted to give them a song that would be of comfort.

LASERLIGHT
Released 13 May 2012

'LaserLight' featured David Guetta and was very different to anything else I'd done before. I wrote it as a thank you for the fans, which the video reflected. It's the last song on the platinum edition, and I thought it was nice to round the album off with a track that was for the Heartbeats. I get a big beam of light from my fans, I get so much love from people, and I wanted to send some love back. As it turned out, it was an amazing way to finish off the album in every sense: a perfect last track and the song that helped me become the first British female to have six number ones on one album. Thanks, David!

Breaking a record was crazy. It was major. I'd always wanted to be in the *Guinness Book of Records*, ever since I was a kid. It was the kind of thing I asked for at Christmas. Being the first female in the UK to have six top-ten singles from the same album in the UK is amazing. That's why the next album needs to have eight top tens on it!

It took about twenty-five minutes to write 'LaserLight'. Sometimes, the instinctual tracks that you don't over-think can be the best. I absolutely love the song now, although it's really hard to sing live. When I'm vocally tired I say, 'YOU SING IT!' to the audience.

It was great to work with David Guetta too – I'm a really big fan of his music. I'd met him at a few events, like the EMAs, and I'd done a track called 'Repeat' for his album *Nothing But The Beat*, so he kindly offered to return the favour. He's such a wicked guy, so talented musically. A musical superhero.

*This picture is
exclusive to the book.*

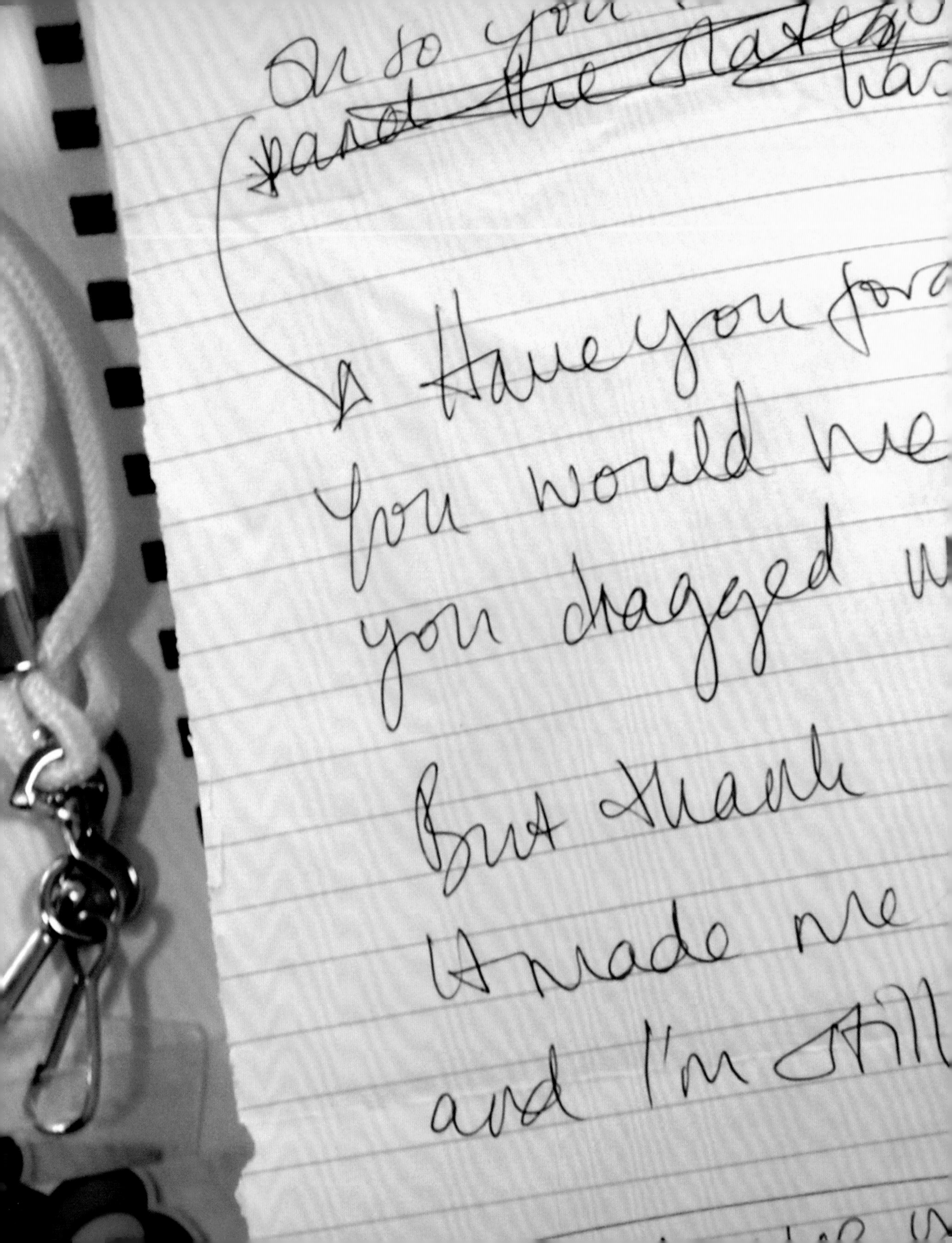

Or so you ~~pant the stateg~~ had

⭐ Have you for
you would me
you dragged

But thank
Amade me
and I'm still

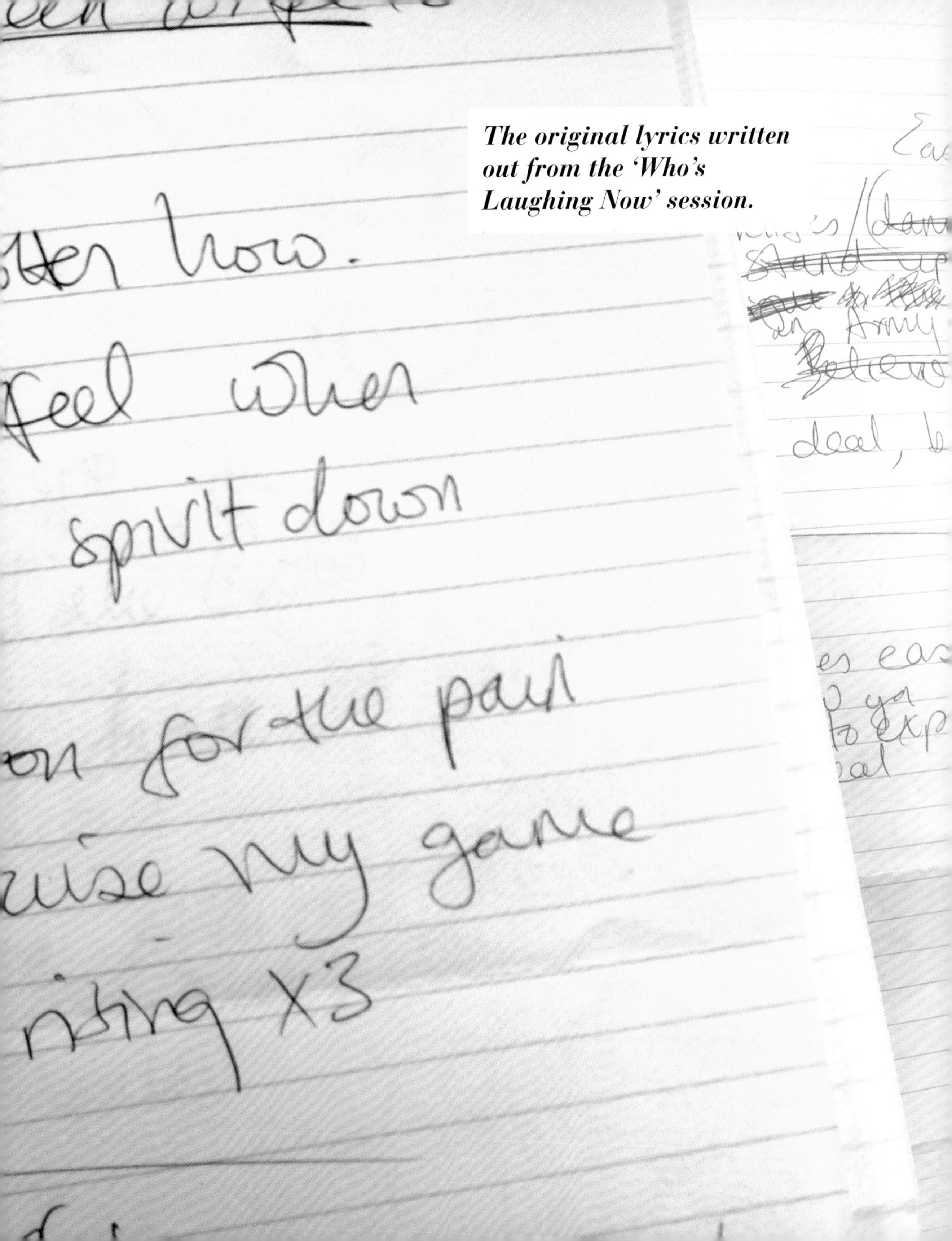

tter now.
feel when
spirit down
on for the pain
uise my game
rising X3

The original lyrics written out from the 'Who's Laughing Now' session.

VIDEOS

DO IT LIKE A DUDE

'Do It Like A Dude' was my first video, and it felt like the longest day of my life. It was a nineteen-hour shoot and my director, Emil Nava, and I just kind of made it up as we went along. It was so much fun, and such an experience because it was so brand new to me. It's funny watching it back and seeing it edited into three minutes when I know how many hours I spent being silly and laughing at myself trying to be manly and G'd up! The spiked lip was a 3am after-thought, and no one realised how much people would love that part of the video. It was what started my obsession with crazy lipstick.

I knew 'Dude' would shock people because it wasn't the norm. I loved that it got people's attention and didn't give everything about me away. It was the perfect combination of POP and mystery.

PRICE TAG

I still have the bear from the video in my living room, he is like part of the family now. This video was so different from 'Dude' and made me realise videos were the perfect opportunity to push boundaries and create everything you can't on stage or in real life. So 'Price Tag' was exactly that. It's still the most watched video I have ever done. :)

NOBODY'S PERFECT

Two days of twenty-hour filming sessions. It was crazy! I absolutely LOVED making this video. I loved showing more of my personality and my different characters, and the visuals were all hand-built in Bulgaria. It blew my mind when I went on set. The cast and costume and lighting were insane. It's still my favourite video to this day.

WHO'S LAUGHING NOW

I had broken my foot after the schedule for the filming for this video had been confirmed, so Emil and I had to adapt the script so that I could be in it even though my foot was still in a cast. It was the funniest video I had done, and it was amazing to share it with the children in the video. I cast the mini Jessie J, Adriana, who is extremely talented and was so professional on set. I loved playing the dinner lady the most – any excuse to pour baked beans over my head has to be a good one!

WHO YOU ARE

This was the hardest video I had done; emotionally, it was hard to hold back the tears because the song means so much to me. I had to focus and really express what the song meant to me, and make sure it spoke to the camera. It was fun doing the rain scene, as I would do it and then have to get dry, redo my hair and go back on set to get completely soaked again. I love how stripped back this video is. Exactly how I wanted it.

DOMINO

I shot 'Domino' in LA, and it was very different to the rest of the videos I had done. It was great to experiment with hair and make-up and just create a really POP-happy, performance-based video.

LASERLIGHT

I enjoyed being girly and more womanly in this video; again I wanted to push boundaries, and show another side of me that my fans hadn't seen. It was freezing and we shot 'LaserLight' in a derelict theatre. What was so amazing about this video was the post-edit, and how much was done with lighting to add to it. It was the first video without the FRINGE (bangs) too!! Waaaaah!!!

*Me and Emil Nava,
my video director,
at the 'LaserLight' video
shoot, 2011.*

CHAPTER FIVE

GOING PLACES

'It's not about the money, money, money // We don't need your money, money, money // We just want to make the world dance // Forget about the price tag...'

Price Tag

It all becomes a whirlwind but what's been amazing writing this book is being able to reflect on how far around the world my music has taken me.

GOING PLACES

WHERE HAVE I BEEN?

AUSTRALIA • *BAHAMAS* • **BELGIUM** • *BRAZIL*
CANADA • *CHINA* • **DUBAI** • *FRANCE* • **GERMANY**
INDONESIA • **IRELAND** • *MALAYSIA* • **NETHERLANDS**
PORTUGAL • **ROMANIA** • *RUSSIA* • **SCOTLAND**
SERBIA • **SINGAPORE** • *SPAIN* • **SWEDEN**
SWITZERLAND • **TURKEY** • *UNITED ARAB EMIRATES*
UNITED KINGDOM • *UNITED STATES* • **WALES**

Here is around 20 per cent of the shows I've done across the world in the past two years and some of the cities I've performed in.

THE LOGIE AWARDS
MELBOURNE

FUTURE MUSIC FESTIVAL
MELBOURNE, SYDNEY, ADELAIDE, BRISBANE

F1 ROCKS
SÃO PAULO

LA FÊTE DE COULEUR
BRUSSELS

MERCEDES SHOW
BEIJING

THE X FACTOR
PARIS

TARATATA
PARIS

AMFAR CHARITY EVENT
CANNES

LE GRAND JOURNAL
CANNES

SHLAG DEN RAAB
BERLIN

TONTRÄGER
MAINZ

THE VOICE
AMSTERDAM

BELGRADE CALLING
BELGRADE

IBIZA LIVE
IBIZA

MAJORCA LIVE
MAJORCA

BENICASSIM
BENICASSIM

THE VOICE
STOCKHOLM

THE MONTREUX JAZZ FESTIVAL
MONTREUX

HEARTBEAT TOUR
SINGAPORE

SUMMER SHOW
ISTANBUL

HORSE RACING WORLD CUP
DUBAI

SOB's
NYC

VIPER ROOM
LA

THE X FACTOR
LA

THE VOICE
LA

KISS FM LIVE
FLORIDA

ELLEN
LA

JAY LENO
LA

CARSON DALY
NYC

SATURDAY NIGHT LIVE
NYC

VH1 DIVAS
NYC

JIMMY KIMMEL
LA

GUESS SHOW
NYC

VIDEO MUSIC AWARDS
LA

ELLE MAGAZINE PARTY
LA

LOS ANGELES - CALIFORNIA
Video MUSIC MTV AWARDS
RADIO FORUM
jessie J
AUGUST 28TH 2011
TALENT
234

GRAHAM NORTON
LONDON

JOOL'S ANNUAL
HOOTENANNY
LONDON

JONATHAN ROSS
LONDON

ALAN CARR
LONDON

SO YOU THINK
YOU CAN DANCE
LONDON

STRICTLY COME
DANCING
LONDON, LIVERPOOL

X FACTOR
LONDON

BRITAIN'S GOT
TALENT
LONDON

BLUE PETER
LONDON

V FEST
*STAFFORDSHIRE,
CHELMSFORD*

WIRELESS
LONDON

RADIO 1's BIG
WEEKEND
HACKNEY, CUMBRIA

GLASTONBURY
GLASTONBURY

STB
WEMBLEY STADIUM

JBB
O2 ARENA

T4 STARS
LONDON

ISLE OF WIGHT
FESTIVAL
ISLE OF WIGHT

BIG CHILL
HEREFORDSHIRE

EMAs
BELFAST

1XTRA
BRIXTON ACADEMY

SHREWSBURY
WARWICK CASTLE
WARWICK

YOYO
NOTTING HILL

ILUVLIVE
LONDON

LAUGHING BOY
LONDON

RADIO 1 LIVE
LOUNGE
LONDON

SCALA
LONDON

KOKO
LONDON

VIVIENNE
WESTWOOD
JEWELLERY
LAUNCH
LONDON

TEENAGE CANCER
TRUST
LONDON

MOBOs
GLASGOW

BRITs LAUNCH
PARTY
LONDON

HEARTBEAT TOUR
*JAKARTA, KUALA
LUMPUR*

It's so crazy seeing the number of people who have put their time and dedication into my live shows over the years. People come and go, but every single person supported me and played an important role in the journey of taking my live shows worldwide. I want to thank everyone who has been involved in making it possible from the beginning.

It takes a huge team to make my shows work, and I am grateful to every single member. To give you an insight into how many people work behind the scenes to make my shows special – from lighting design to set building, from sound guys to wardrobe – here is my current travelling team:

THE TEAM

MANAGEMENT Crown Management – Mark Hargreaves and Lily Crockford, the most wonderful management I have ever had. Thank you for believing in me and letting me be me.

AGENT Creative Artists Agency – Paul Franklin.

TOUR MANAGEMENT John Pryer and Cez Darke.

PRODUCTION MANAGEMENT John Pryer.

PRODUCTION ASSISTANT Gemma Peacock.

FRONT OF HOUSE SOUND Chris Madden.

MONITORS Jon Lewis.

LIGHTING DESIGNER Vince Foster.

SET DESIGN John Pryer.

SECURITY Mark Dawson.

MUSICAL DIRECTOR Kojo Samuel.

DRUMS Ginger Hamilton.

KEYS Hannah Vasanth.

GUITAR Lewis Allen.

BASS Phil Simmonds.

BACKING VOCALS Cherise Voncelle and Phebe Edwards.

HAIR Alisha Dobson and Lyndell Mansfield.

MAKE-UP Myself, Karin Darnell and Andrew Gilmore.

NAILS Jenny Longworth.

This is me and Mark, my manager, in LA in 2011.

FOUR RANDOM STORIES

LA

The hardest gig of my life was the Clive Davis party for the pre-Grammys in LA in 2012. I was booked to perform with Monica and Brandy to do a Diana Ross tribute. I'm such a huge fan of both of those women; their vocals have had a huge influence on me.

Whitney wanted to meet me at the party; Sunday 11 February was the day I was going to be meeting Whitney Houston. I was also singing 'Who You Are' and 'Domino' at the party and was so excited for her to hear me sing them, as 'Domino' was hugely influenced by her music.

As we were getting ready in my hotel room (my room was next to Alicia Keys, Monica and Brandy, and Whitney's room was right down the hall), I remember my manager, Mark, phoning my hair assistant, Alisha, who was with me at the time; she just went, 'Oh my God, oh my God, OK.' She told me that Whitney Houston had literally just passed away. I heard it, but I didn't believe it. I couldn't understand what she was telling me at all; it didn't make any sense. You think these people are invincible.

I was put in the hardest position, because they asked if I still wanted to perform. Of course I wanted to, in her honour, but it didn't feel right. The party was in the same hotel she had just passed away in. There were more people at the party that night because of what had happened than there would have been if she hadn't died. I think everybody wanted to be part of a night to celebrate her life.

The more I think about it, the weirder it is. I thought I was going to meet her that evening, but instead I ended up singing in her honour. It was so strange. I remember saying on stage, 'Whitney's the person who made me feel comfortable with having a loud, powerful voice.' We've got hundreds of videos of me mimicking her when I was four years old: 'I Will Always Love You', 'Saving All My Love For You' – I used to sing that song over and over and over again.

I still don't believe it, to be honest. I was so emotional and so scared and so sad. I walked into the room and everyone was there – Diddy, Kelly Rowland, Erykah Badu, India Arie... Everyone was there. I went on stage, and I just went for it. She was still there in a weird kind of way. It was a strange and emotional evening, one I will never forget.

KUALA LUMPUR

I had one of the best days of my life earlier this year in Kuala Lumpur, at the end of my Asian tour. I got up at 7.30am and wrote a great song that's going to be on the second album. Then I went to the gym – felt ready for the day. It was boiling and there was a slide into the pool. My excitement was ridiculous, haha!

My band and I had a BBQ by the pool for lunch after swimming for a bit. Then we went to do the sound check for the gig, which was inside a drained swimming pool in a theme park. After sound check we had two hours to go and explore the theme park. We went on roller coasters, and those swan ride things that go in the water, LOL. We also walked the biggest free-standing bridge in the world. It was EPIC! I was like, yeah, I can do this. As we started to walk across, I started to freak out as it was so high. I started sweating and laughing whilst crying. It took us about fifteen minutes and all of us were equally as freaked out. But it was such a feeling of satisfaction making it to the other side, we were all so proud of each other. The gig was the best on the tour and Tinie and his people came down as they were in town doing a show the next day. We all hung out after the gig and celebrated a great day.

MAJORCA/IBIZA

I recently went to Ibiza for the first time. I did two shows, two sets, two flights, two islands, twelve songs, two outfits, one hairstyle, all in the space of twenty-four hours. I started in Ibiza, then flew to Majorca and performed there at 10.30pm to a very hyped, incredible crowd – the first show in almost a year without my band. Then I got a jet back to Ibiza, where I performed at 3.30am in a club to an equally hyped crowd! BOOM! The sound wasn't great at first but the audience were amazingly understanding while we worked it out. Mark Wright turned up and was getting lots of attention while I was on stage, sweating like crazy, singing 'Domino'. Lavely!

GLASGOW/ SCOTLAND MOBOS

The MOBO Awards were the first time I had ever opened an award ceremony. The pressure to start the party was huge! With all the artists sitting around the stage, I felt the buzz start to take over and I just wanted to perform the best I ever had. I had three outfits for the night, why not? One for the red carpet, one for the 'Dude' performance and then a catsuit for the rest of the night. The red carpet was fun, my fans were there in full strength and I was laughing to myself the whole time, as my dress was very 'red carpet' but my shoes were DMs.

I was so nervous because it was the first major performance I did after my cast had been removed from my ankle. I was a little on the skinny side and could only hop. Sad times. The reaction when people saw the Jessie J lookalike was amazing, it was my idea and I wanted people to understand what the song was about. Pushing her off stage was me taking the mickey out of myself. I remember shouting out, 'Tinie, Chip, listen!' before I sang, 'Boys, come, come, say what you wanna!' That wasn't planned, I was just ad-libbing and they were the two people I could see. I also remember randomly singing that part in a really deep squat. Nice!

I was nominated for four awards that night and had no idea if I had a chance at winning. I was sitting right next to the stage and someone in my team said, 'That's always a good sign.' My mum and dad were there, my best friend Holly was sat next to me, and my label and management were too. When my name was called for the first award and I realised I had won, I was in complete shock. Then after the second, third and then finally winning BEST UK ACT as the fourth award, I was almost lost for words! I don't even remember what I said in my speech. When I came off stage and had to do the press run I just cried, I was so humbled by the support of my fans and the MOBOs. It still doesn't feel real now. I look at the awards at home and feel so thankful.

When you're travelling constantly and you rarely have time to come up for air, it all becomes a whirlwind, but what's been amazing about writing this book is being able to reflect on how far around the world my music has taken me. I feel so blessed to be able to meet different fans from so many different countries and see places that are simply unforgettable.

Crazy to think that's only in the first eighteen months. I am so looking forward to seeing where my music will take me next on my travels. The unknown is often the most beautiful. I can't wait.

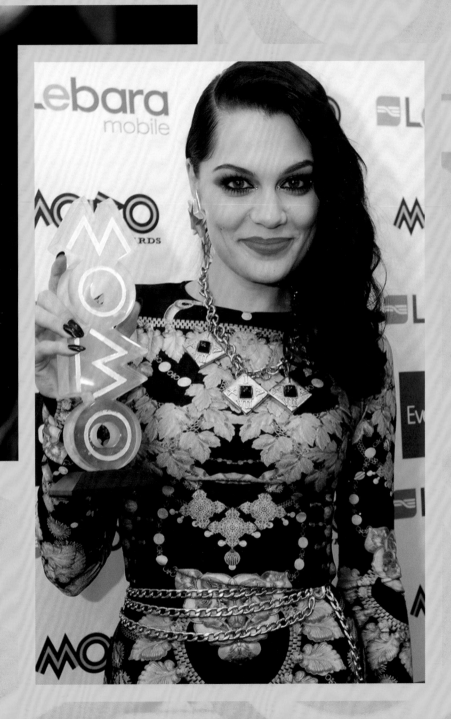

CHAPTER SIX

LOVE & HATE

'Just follow the beat, the rhythm will lead you right back to me...'

CASUALTY OF LOVE

They love me, they love me not,
they love me, they love me not, they love me,
they love me not, they love me,
they love me not…

LOVE

The people I admire most in the world are my mum and dad. They've supported me in my career, they have always been there for me, but above all, they've shown me what love is. They've been married for thirty-five years and they still go on dates. I look at them and feel so happy I've been brought up in a family that was built on such a solid foundation of love.

What is love to me? Now that's a huge question, and I've learnt to protect my heart and keep it private, as it's no one's business but my own; in this life you have to hold onto the things that are private. I'm still trying to find my feet in love. I have learnt a lot about myself in the last few years and I have matured. I feel in my generation we want to experience love so badly; we are desperate to experience it, so we force it.

I think love is when you don't even realise it's happening. It's just something that feels right. I remember my dad saying to me, 'If there were certain things that your mum hadn't changed or I hadn't changed about myself, then we wouldn't be together now.' I think it's an understanding that you have to adapt. You're never going to fit perfectly with someone, and you shouldn't, because we are forever evolving and changing and growing. Life doesn't stand still and neither does love.

I'm ready to accept that I want to welcome love into my life one day, on the right day. Love that I deserve and love on love's terms – nothing else. It would be nice to have someone to share my life with. But when the time is right, it will happen.

Music is where I let myself go and write what's really in my heart, so there isn't much else to say. Just that I love right and I love good.

PRESS

I remember seeing myself in a magazine for the first time, it was so weird! I was like, 'Mum, look, I'm in *RWD* magazine!' I remember when I was in the *Metro*, a paper I had read every day going to The BRIT School on the train.

I have a book of all the magazine shoots and newspaper articles about me, and I often read it to remind myself of how amazing it's been and still is. In fact it's rare that there is negative press, but they are always the stories that create more of a hype than the positive press, sadly.

> ## " I HAVE A BOOK OF ALL THE MAGAZINE SHOOTS AND NEWSPAPER ARTICLES ABOUT ME "

I remember experiencing the press being mean to me for the first time – it's hard to get used to. There is no practice run.

When people believe a false story and start to judge you about something that's untrue, it's out of your control and it sucks. It's a lovely thing, though, when something is written about you in a positive and true light, and there have been more of those stories than negative ones.

I have always been extremely honest and tried to make sure my fans always have a clear understanding of who I am. That way, they can always see the difference in a true or a false story; sometimes it's not that easy though.

I have been overwhelmed by the amount of support I have received from magazines and the majority of newspapers in the last two years, across the world. It's mind blowing, especially how they celebrated what I wanted to bring to the music world.

I was so busy in the beginning, and more often than not in the early stages of a new career the UK press are supportive and excited. From best dressed to worst dressed, from a good review to a bad review, it was all amazing and it still is now. But, when it gets to a point where there is not much new stuff left to write about the music, that's when you start seeing the 'make up anything' stories. We all love them... NOT!

I remember my first experience of being papped, it was crazy. I couldn't see – you have to just walk, you can't stop or they swarm you. It's so easy for them to get the 'eye half shut' picture, because unless you look down or really focus you genuinely can't see s***! To put it bluntly.

I was scared the first time I got followed by five cars and three motorbikes. It was the first time I was number one, with 'Price Tag', and it was the way they were driving that scared me the most, cutting up cars and going through red lights, banging on my car window. I actually cried – it was late at night, it was raining, and I just wanted to go home, but they refused to leave me alone unless I got out of the car and posed for a picture. My best friend said, 'There is no turning back now.' The moments like that, which most people don't get to see, are the hardest bits.

The paps are hardcore – not all of them are, I guess, but for a woman, if you take the camera away, it's just a man lying on the ground, looking up your skirt. But because he has a camera, he calls it a job. How that's legal is beyond me. I understand they want to get a look at my outfit, that it is about getting that shot of me arriving at an event... It's all part of the job, but it's when I'm not at work and they're still trying to pap me – that's when it

bothers me. Not everyone I am with or hang out with wants to be pictured, and there might just be times when I don't want to be seen, when things are private. I suppose it's those experiences that have taught me that I have to have secrets, and it's OK not to give everything away. I used to, but I don't anymore – you have to keep something back for your sanity. Everybody deserves their privacy.

I don't know why some of the press try and sabotage people instead of celebrating those who are successful. They build you up and rip you down, without considering that it's not a game – it's people's lives. I look at someone like Amy Winehouse, and I always think that the love she received when she had sadly passed away was the love she needed when she was alive, especially from the press. It was the same with Whitney Houston, and with Michael Jackson.

The media have got a lot to do with the way people look at anyone, including artists. You can't control what they write and it's so frustrating when it's negative or untrue. When the media do write a positive story in a true light, it's wonderful. You feel like, even if you haven't met someone, they are understanding what you're about and getting to know the real you.

I could list a thousand things I want to set straight, but the truth is I know the truth and that's all that matters. I have a wonderful PR team at Purple PR, in Carl Fysh and Emma Philpot. They have taught me so much since day one. Thank you! :)

DIVA

What does 'diva' mean anymore? When I was growing up, 'diva' to me meant big hair, big voice, extravagant clothes, long nails, epic songs, amazing make-up and a BIG career. With a dash of princess behaviour (sometimes).

When I think 'diva', I think of artists like Diana Ross, Shirley Bassey, Whitney Houston and Tina Turner, and of how I was always trying to mimic them at home in front of the mirror. With their music blaring, wearing the showiest clothes I could find and drowning in my mum's jewellery, with lipstick all over my face. Now I'm grown up, it seems that having the word 'diva' attached to your name can be a negative in many ways.

So here it is... I want to tell you the FULL story of the first time I was called a (dun dun duuuuuun) *DIVA*. *Finger snap, hair flick*.

I was in Australia, and had been promoting 'Price Tag' across the US, Canada, Australia and New Zealand for almost four months. I was getting an average of about four hours' sleep a night and I was a little emotionally and physically drained to say the least. I missed home a lot.

I had no clean clothes and, for any girl, an event like a red-carpet event is one you prepare for months for. I had nothing left to wear so it was a situation of work with what you got, or go naked with your clothes painted on.

So I tried to be some Gok Wan character and create a red carpet dress with an American Apparel swimming costume (yes, it starts bad and only gets worse), a wire see-through black maxi dress, a fake-fur waistcoat and tights that made me look like a pencil.

My fringe had grown out and I decided to cut it. Just a word of advice: *don't attempt to cut your fringe yourself when you're stressed, tired and have twenty minutes to get ready for a red carpet, it's going to go wrong*. Which it did. I cut my fringe half way up my head; taking an eyebrow off with it only added to the humour of the outfit I had already created. Then I thought, I will do a sexy smoky eye, maybe it will distract from everything else. Again, can you tell I was alone in this hotel room? There was no one to tell me I was about to step into a situation where everyone else looked like a princess and I looked like a witch about to cast a spell.

I am joking about it all now, but at the time the pressure of styling myself, doing my own hair and make-up, hardly sleeping and knowing I was going to have cameras taking pictures of me from every angle was stressful – it would be for any girl. I had a moment of, 'I can't do it!' and I remember sitting on the bathroom floor, crying hysterically amongst the hair from my fringe. Like a scene from *EastEnders*. *Expecting Peggy to roll in with a set of curlers and save me*. That didn't happen, so it was down to me to pull myself together and do my job.

I rang my mum, and she calmed me down, told me it's OK to have moments like that. We

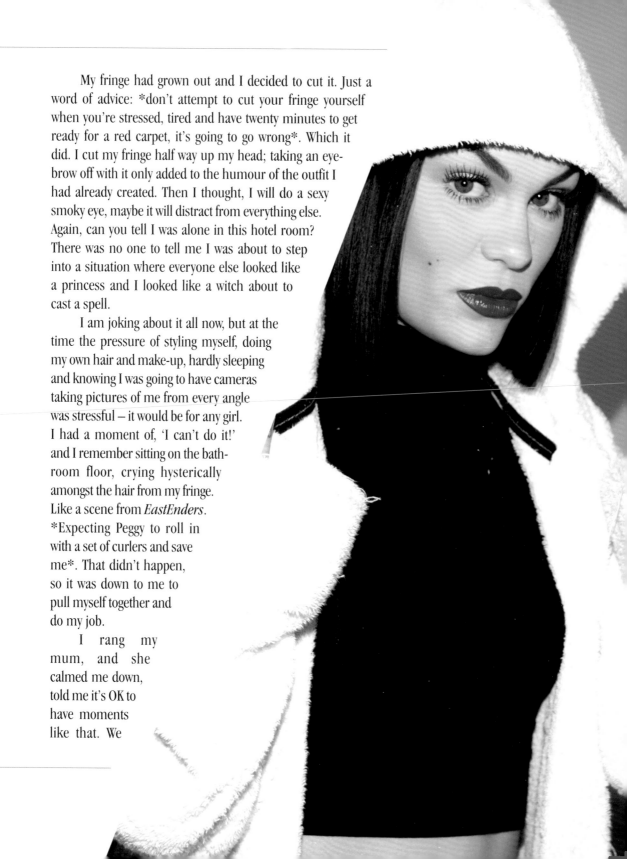

all reach boiling point sometimes, she said, and she told me to take a deep breath, stop crying and start again. I stopped crying, re-did my make-up and prepared myself for a red carpet wearing a SWIMMING COSTUME! (It's OK, you can laugh.)

I won't pretend that there aren't moments when I have to work and I don't want to. It's normal to have days like that. I had asked politely if I could miss the red carpet so I could sleep before my performance, as I would rather be mentally ready to sing over anything else. I was told, no, you have to do it.

I was thirty minutes late and considering the state both my hotel room and I were in, I don't think that was too bad. I was aware there were about ten people outside my dressing room stressing and bitching – not because I'm paranoid, but because I could hear them. One woman said, 'I don't even like her music to be honest and now I'm waiting for her.' And then I heard it: 'Ugh, she is such a DIVA!' I opened my door instantly and said, 'Hello, OK, so I am ready', fighting back the tears and the urge to say something. But I always keep my cool. Most of the time. ;)

The two women who had obviously been talking about me were nice as pie. They were all, 'Wow you look amazing!' 'So lovely to meet you!' I apologised for being late and as I walked to the red carpet I closed my eyes and thought back to myself as a little girl, singing Whitney Houston songs in the mirror. That will always be the meaning of 'diva' to me.

ARQIVA COMMERCIAL RADIO AWARDS 2012 PPL BREAKTHROUGH
UK Artist of the Year

BBC SOUND OF 2011 *Winner*

BRIT AWARDS 2011 *Critic's Choice*

BT DIGITAL MUSIC AWARDS 2011
*Best Newcomer; Best Female Artist;
Best Song ('Price Tag')*

COSMO 2011 *Music Artist of the Year*

CAPITAL FM AWARDS 2011
Best Role Model in Pop

GLAMOUR AWARDS 2011
Woman of Tomorrow

GLAMOUR AWARDS 2012 *UK Solo Artist*

HARPER'S BAZAAR WOMEN OF THE YEAR AWARDS 2011
Breakthrough of the Year

MOBO AWARDS 2011
*Best Newcomer; Best UK Act;
Best Album ('Who You Are');
Best Song ('Do It Like A Dude')*

MTV VIDEO PLAY AWARDS 2012
'Price Tag' 2x Platinum

POPCRUSH MUSIC AWARDS 2011
Best New Artist

Q AWARDS 2011
Best Video ('Do It Like A Dude')

SILVER CLEF AWARDS 2012
Best British Act

URBAN MUSIC AWARDS 2011
Best Female Artist

VIRGIN MEDIA AWARDS 2011
Best Newcomer

BREAK A LEG

'Do It Like A Dude' had gone to number two and 'Price Tag' to number one, and I started to get all of these messages from different artists. I was tweeted by my fans that Britney Spears, Missy Elliott and Justin Bieber had said they were fans.

I felt like a whole other world was tapping into what I was doing. It's always nice to receive compliments from the very people you listened to growing up. Erykah Badu tweeted me once. I just stared at it. Amazing.

It kept me pushing on, because one single going to number one doesn't mean you've made it; I like to work hard for success so it gave me even more reason to push harder.

FOOT FIRST

So, I'd had a number one single, my career was is in a great place, and my album *Who You Are* was flying off the shelves. I was ready to rock the summer and I was booked to play every major festival. Then I had an accident that would change everything.

I was filming for an advert and was asked to stand on a revolving platform. As the platform began to move, I lost my balance and fell off. My left foot went inwards while my leg was still straight and there was this horrible snapping sound as it cracked. Gross. It was so quick, and it's crazy because I had joked as I arrived, 'I bet I fall off that and break my foot or something.'

Straight away, I knew I'd broken it. 'I have broken my ankle, I have broken my ankle!' – that's all I could say.

My mum and dad had come down to see me and were watching me film the advert, so luckily they were there to hold my hand. They were as shocked as I was, I was just trying not to faint from the pain and my jean shorts were so uncomfortable – the things you remember are so random!

I sat back onto the floor as someone took my shoe off and four men had to hold my leg up in the air, as my foot had started to go purple, like a mini Barney the Dinosaur. (You will begin to see I am obsessed with all things miniature.)

They rushed me to A & E in an ambulance. I refused pain relief and the ambulance guy just could not understand why. I don't like needles so I was trying to style it out, but I failed. LOL. I gave in, eventually.

If you're in an ambulance, you're legally required to go through A & E, so when I was being taken through, people were filming me on their phones while I was sitting in agony. That's the kind of thing I don't like. The last thing you want is people taking your photo or uploading a video of you crying to the Internet. I will never get used to that.

The nurse came out and said I would need X-rays to be sure of the injury. After the X-ray, it was a waiting game. The doctor came with the results after about two hours *drum roll please* and said, 'We couldn't see any breaks so it must be a bad sprain. Can I have an autograph for my wife?' It was a real split between relief because it wasn't broken and worry because I didn't know if I believed him.

I had sprained my left ankle before and I knew it wasn't the same, but I just wanted to get out of there to be honest. I felt like an animal in a cage – even the nurses were taking pictures of me. People were staring and shouting things out, and I was just waiting patiently for the painkillers to kick in. They gave me crutches and some tight sock thing and sent me on my way. You should've seen the first time I tried to use the crutches. Some kind of Bambi character.

The day after it happened, I was booked to perform at the Capital Summertime Ball in front of 75,000 people, the first time I would play Wembley Stadium.

I had the medical on-site doctor come and look at my foot as, apparently, he was a foot specialist. He took one look at it and said, 'That's definitely not a sprain, it's probably a severely torn ligament.' (Bear in mind he had been told that it wasn't broken.) He advised me to go home. I didn't. Actually, if I remember correctly, my reply was, 'F*?k it, it's Wembley Stadium, I have performed sitting down before, I can do it again!'

I went on stage with a Claire's Accessories sock on my foot (loving it) – to this day people still think it was a cast. It wasn't, it was actually just a sock because my foot was so swollen. It

> " **YOU SHOULD HAVE SEEN THE FIRST TIME I TRIED TO USE CRUTCHES. SOME KIND OF BAMBI CHARACTER** "

was so freakin' painful. I was fully dosed-up on painkillers and, to be honest, I don't even remember performing – it was all a bit of a blur. I remember the audience singing 'Price Tag' and it giving me major goosebumps.

So it was obviously very lastminute.com, but we hired some dancers, got a throne and sat me down on it! I don't regret doing it – it was one of the best gigs of my career. The way the crowd made me feel welcome and cared for was so nice.

My next mission was the repack for my deluxe version of *Who You Are*. I had been given two or three weeks to write some new material, and the day after the Summertime Ball I was booked to go to LA to write with Claude Kelly and Dr. Luke. I was told not to fly, but everyone told me I had to. So I packed all the right feet to my shoes and some Claire's Accessories socks. LOL.

I flew to LA, but when I landed my foot was double its size. It was green and purple and looked like it was related to Shrek. It was the hardest studio session; I know myself, and I can push through colds and pains and stomach ache, but this – this was a different league of pain. I was in the studio ice-ing my foot but it seemed to be doing nothing. I was just so worried, and as the days went by I knew it wasn't a sprain.

A few days after landing in LA, I spent a few hours listening to old-school Whitney and Prince with Claude and Luke, to cheer myself up. I said I wanted to do a feel-good song like 'I Wanna Dance With Somebody' or 'Kiss', and Luke started playing a guitar lick that

would later be the main hook line for 'Domino'. Amazing. Writing the lyrics for 'Domino' was so natural, recording it was the challenge, as I did the whole song sitting down and with my leg raised on ice. Weird vision, but I focused on the words and the music and tried to take myself out of what I felt at the time. Which was not 'sexy and free'. It was and still is one of my favourite songs I have recorded and co-written. It just makes me feel good.

Flying home was hard, I had been in LA for a week and my foot was so painful and swollen and green that I had told my management at the time that I refused to continue working until I saw a specialist. I had to put myself first.

So I went to see a specialist on Harley Street, took my sock off and showed him my foot. He took one look at it and said, 'OK, we need to start all over again. Pretend you did it an hour ago.' I had an X-ray and a CT scan that very day and the specialist said it had become a lot worse because it had been left so long. He looked at the scans and told me *drum roll please* I had, in fact, broken it twice on the joint and would possibly need surgery. I was shocked, but also angry at myself for knowing it wasn't a sprain and not doing something about it sooner.

He called me that night and said, in a rather serious tone, 'If you don't have this operation, there's a good chance you won't walk properly ever again.' That's when my stomach dropped. But then, if I hadn't gone to LA, would I have written 'Domino'?

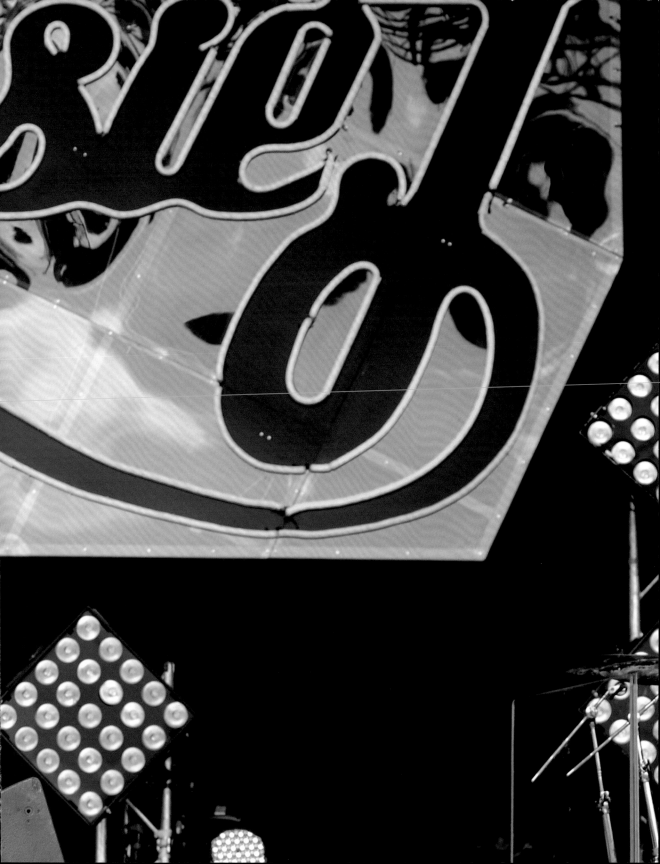

The double-sided sword of the industry.

The doctor booked me in for surgery the following Thursday. I was told I would need four to six weeks just to recover from the surgery. No one is prepared for that kind of news, and in my diary there is never space to be hurt or sick, so I knew I was going to be letting people down. I had to cancel a lot of events that I was booked for and a lot of personal things too. I was heartbroken. I had a moment of 'Why now?' But then the realist in me kicked in and I was thinking how lucky I was that it wasn't worse. I had to prepare myself for the surgery and not think about what I was missing out on. Getting better was the priority.

I had a very serious business meeting with my management to discuss how we would go about announcing that I wouldn't be performing at the festivals – a lot of thought has to go into something like that, as sometimes people twist the truth.

It was also my chance, once again, to prove to myself that those kinds of things don't hold me back. As it turned out, I cancelled only six shows. I did as much as I could, even when I probably shouldn't have.

The surgery was horrible. One of my biggest fears is general anesthetic. As I was put under I was singing 'Who You Are' really fast, like some sort of hospital remix. I don't remember anything until coming around and being sick straight away. I burst into tears and held my mum's hand. I was just glad I had got through it.

The doc came in and explained it was even worse than he had thought – when opening my ankle up he discovered the bone had gone like a crunchie bar (yes the chocolate bar, vomit) and he couldn't save it. He had to reconstruct my whole ankle joint. No wonder it hurt. So I was given a fusion and bone transplant, a metal plate and four screws. Blinged my ankle bone out nicely, Doc.

I couldn't get out of bed after I'd had the surgery. Watching daytime TV isn't exactly my kind of thing but I had to lie flat for about two weeks, with my left leg raised. If my mum hadn't been there, I wouldn't have eaten or washed. My ankle was too painful to move. My mum cared for me, and my dad and my sisters and my good, good friends came around and helped out. You really find out who your real friends are through something like that.

The media reaction was really supportive when it was announced I was cancelling shows. A lot of my fans were too, but as always you get a handful who are not. That wasn't easy. People tweeting me saying 'You b****, how dare you not perform. You've broken your leg, so what.' There was no way I could have done those shows. I never expect everyone to care or understand, but I do ask that people remember I am human too. It was physically impossible, I had to recover from the surgery.

Since my foot has healed I have undergone very little physio due to my demanding diary, but it's getting there. I'm just making sure it gets some TLC.

FAMILY FIRST

It can all get surreal – magical – but surreal. My family are my rock, my everything. Anyone who is close to me knows that being a daughter, a sister, a sister-in-law, Auntie Jess and a granddaughter is as important and as equal as me being Jessie J. I have other roles in my life that I love, as well as performing and working.

I have two nephews and one niece, and they are my world. The love I feel for them is unreal. It's not easy for them to come and visit me at work and when they do I get frustrated that all my attention can't just be on them. I love to crawl around with them on the floor, pretending to be a dinosaur. I'm Auntie Jess to all of them, not Jessie J.

Being with them makes me realise how funny and normal my family is, how blessed and lucky I am to have them as my family. We are very free in our humour and the way we are with each other. People meet me and say, 'Why are you the way you are?' Then they meet my mum and my dad and my sisters and my brother-in-laws, and it all makes sense. We're so similar; we just love to have fun and make each other laugh. We're the sanest yet craziest family you'll meet.

CHAPTER SEVEN

BEHIND THE SCENES

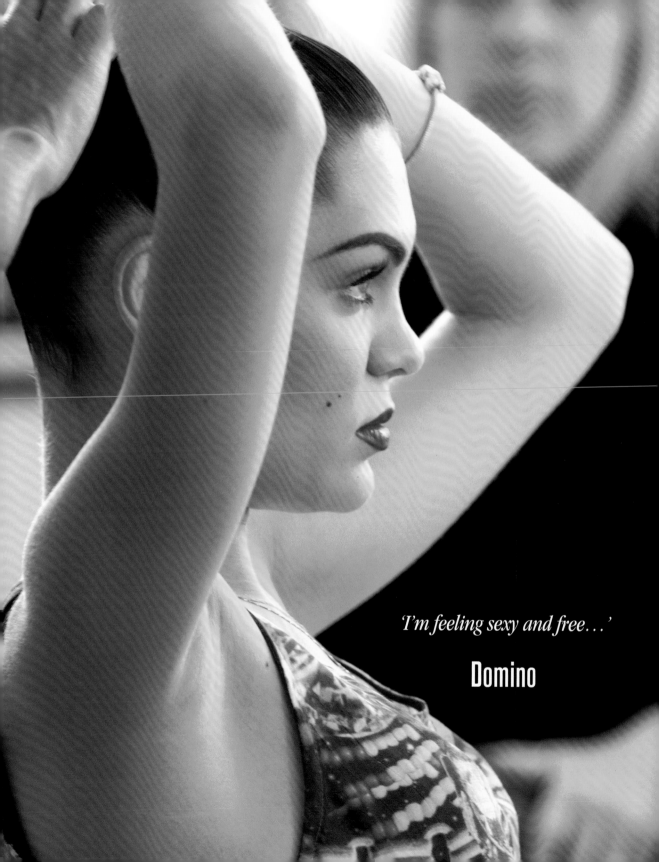

'I'm feeling sexy and free…'

Domino

People always get to see the end product of
a photo shoot, but what you don't get to see is what
happens behind the scenes. Doing shoots is one of the
best parts of the job; I love getting to experiment and
a big part of what I do is expressing myself through
clothes, hair, nails and make-up.

Doing the shoot for this book was particularly great –
and I'm not just saying that, it was – I had creative
control over my look so I loved it. I had fun with it
because it was so relaxed. I think we managed to get the
'classic Jessie poses' that everyone likes.

Sometimes you can walk onto a set for a magazine or
promo shoot and it's so stale; they treat you like you're
a model and forget that you're actually an artist who's
just getting dressed up and having her photo taken.
Being a singer is very different from being a model.
As so much of what I do now, it's about
learning as I go.

Strike a pose ;)

SHOOT
SCHEDULE

8.30: Photographer and crew arrive to set up. The photographer today is the incredible Simon Emmett.

9.00: My team arrives to sort out all the clothes and make-up. The dressing room is full of lipsticks, catsuits and shoes.

10.00: I arrive at Spring Studios in London's Kentish Town, and enjoy a breakfast of eggs and toast. I love my food, and I can't work properly if I don't eat breakfast. Grumpy Jess comes out.

10.15: I talk through the different looks of the day with the stylist. There's always a lot to choose from. Today we wanted a mixture of fun, casual looks and then something to contrast with that — me all dressed up and ready to take on the world. Among the choices are thirteen belts, twelve necklaces, House of Holland for Pretty Polly tights, Wolford, a vintage Yves Saint Laurent shirt, a Dolce & Gabbana sequinned jacket and a top from Sass & Bide.

10.30: Hair and make-up time. Usually I like to do my own make-up, but when it's a day like today, and we have so much to do, I ask Andrew Gallimore or Karin Darnell to come and help me out. Today I have the amazing Karin.

13.02: We shoot 'Look One'. I know two-and-a-half hours seems a long time to get ready. If I'm at home or hanging out with friends, then it takes me a little less time. Like today, I got to the shoot with no make-up, my hair a mess and wearing Diesel jeans and some leather Converse. In my own time, I love to be really comfortable! With a shoot, you have to make sure your make-up is good with the lights and the heat, my hair needs to work with what I'm wearing, and so on. It's really time-consuming, to be honest, but you have to get it right. Strike another pose!

14.14: Lunch, and time for some Moroccan lamb, salad and chicken. Shhpicey!

14.52: Back to it. We're on 'Look Three' by now. One thing I'm grateful for is that I tend to get the right picture really quickly. Sometimes a photographer will request two hours, but after an hour it's like, 'Done!' Changing outfits and redoing my hair is what takes time; once I'm in front of the camera, we can easily do a whole look in half an hour, tops.

16.48: We're done. We photographed four different looks plus the cover shot in about two hours – if you subtract the time for lunch and getting glammed.

17.10: The day isn't over yet. Once the book shoot is finished, there are pictures to take for the tour promo, then I need to film promo clips to announce my new Nice To Meet You tour, do some book promo, and finally a quick interview.

> ❝ ONCE THE BOOK SHOOT IS FINISHED, THERE ARE PICTURES TO TAKE FOR THE TOUR **PROMO** ❞

20.48: No, still not done. Though it's time to leave Spring Studios – I'm starving and needing a Nando's right now (butter-fried chicken, medium, macho peas, halloumi cheese, fries or rice, if you're wondering!) – I have international phone interviews to do, paperwork to sign and meetings to prepare for the next day. By the time I get to bed, it'll be well past midnight, but it's all part of the job. Go hard, or go home!

SHOOT PLAYLIST

Here is what I listened to while shooting the pictures for this very book. From old-school classics to throwback soul, there were also plenty of my favourite tunes from this year too. Photo shoots can be really long, so a good playlist is vital – it keeps you going when you get tired and just want to lie down and sleep.

'All The Man That I Need'
WHITNEY HOUSTON

'In For The Kill'
LA ROUX

'Watch 'n' Learn'
RIHANNA

'Skinny Love'
BIRDY

'I Can't See
Myself Leaving You'
ARETHA FRANKLIN

'Empire State Of Mind'
JAY-Z FT. ALICIA KEYS

'Fast Car'
TRACY CHAPMAN

'I Used To Love Him'
*LAURYN HILL FT.
MARY J. BLIGE*

'Past My Shades'
B.o.B FT. LUPE FIASCO

'LaserLight'
JESSIE J

'Yellow'
COLDPLAY

'Beautiful People'
CHRIS BROWN

'Got To Get You Into My Life'
EARTH, WIND & FIRE

'Where Do
We Go From Here?'
ALICIA KEYS

'All In Me'
BRANDY

'HYFR'
DRAKE FT. LIL WAYNE

'Moves Like Jagger'
*MAROON 5 FT.
CHRISTINA AGUILERA*

'Cater 2 U'
DESTINY'S CHILD

'Real Love'
MARY J. BLIGE

'Pass Out'
TINIE TEMPAH

'Soldier of Love'
SADE

*Another picture
exclusive to the book.*

GET THE LOOK

WHAT I WORE
Here's what I wore on the shoot.

LOOK ONE:
Sheer cropped top – Krystof Strozyna
Black bra – Calvin Klein
Black leather shorts – Helen Steele
'Jessie' necklace – my own
Gold chain bracelets – my own
Hoop earrings – Topshop

LOOK TWO:
Studded denim jacket – Ragged Priest
Lion body – Black Milk
Black leather shorts – Helen Steele

LOOK THREE:
White cropped T-shirt – Dolce & Gabbana
Tie-dye denim shorts – Ragged Priest,
    customised by Wendy Benstead
Powder blue boots – Jeffrey Campbell
Aztec-style hoop earrings – Kokon To Zai

LOOK FOUR:
Black crop top – American Apparel
Black pants – American Apparel
Black boots – Giuseppe Zanotti
Vintage gold necklaces – Susan Caplan and
    Liz Mendez Vintage

'Jessie' necklace – my mum had it made
for me.

MY LOOK

I've definitely softened my look recently. I'm not so much a fan of the bob and dark lips and all that stuff anymore. I see it as a look, but not one for every day. It's too harsh on me now. My face has changed shape – I've actually lost a lot of weight in my face. If you look at pictures from two years ago, I was a bit chubbier in the face back then.

It's so important not to be scared to experiment with your hair and make-up, and different looks. Just have fun with it. Never listen to people when they say, 'I don't like your hair like that, Jessie' or 'That make-up is too soft on you'. It's about doing what you want, and enjoying it while you do.

So, who knows, maybe one day I will rock double denim – unlikely, but you never know! I sometimes don't even trust myself.

It's not only my style that has changed. I look back at the early Jessie J videos and, let's face it, I used to be addicted to blusher. My mum actually sat me down once and said, 'I need to talk to you about something serious…' I was so worried, all these terrible thoughts rushed through my head. 'Jess, you wear way too much blusher.' The way she dropped it was so real that for a time I was scared of blusher and I went a bit too pale. I think I've now found a happy medium. I love lipstick too; I'm into Angelique Beige Dior lipstick. I wear it pretty much every day. It's been funny to see how what I wear has this massive effect on sales. Whatever I say I'm wearing sells out so quickly. American Apparel across the whole of the UK sold out of their disco pants after I wore them on *Graham Norton*. And an ASOS dress that I wore on *The Voice* also sold out hours after me wearing it. I buy my own things though; people always assume I get freebies but not as often as you think.

FASHION Q&A

I HAVE COMMITTED FASHION FAUX PAS...

My teeth at the first BRITs launch were redonkuloso – they looked like baby sweetcorn, they were so yellow. It was so gross. I have had them whitened since.

WHEN IT COMES TO REAL FUR v FAKE FUR...

It's fake fur every time. I'm very anti-fur. It's just wrong. If you watch documentaries about how they produce fur, it's unbelievable and so unnecessary. A lot of artists I know wear fur, and I tell them to educate themselves on where the fur they're wearing comes from. If you're going to wear it, at least know what you're doing.

SOMEONE I CONSIDER A STYLE ICON IS...

Gwen Stefani. Gwen has been cool for years and she'll stay cool for years. I'll be honest, there's no one in particular that I can pick out in the UK.

ONE KEY THING TO DRESSING WELL AS A WOMAN...

... is doing what you want to do and not what everyone else is doing. Always be comfortable for whatever event you're going to, whether it's the park or a wedding. Just feel ultra sensual and sexy and beautiful in your own way.

A TREND I PERSONALLY DON'T HAVE TIME FOR IS...

... fake Uggs. The ones that walk next to girls' feet. The way they scuff on the floor. Nah mate!

THE LAST FREEBIE I RECEIVED WAS...

... a really adorable iPhone cover from Moschino. Thanks, I love it!

I'LL WEAR HIGH STREET TO BOND STREET...

I've always said that style shouldn't have a brand. I think style should come from you. Whether it's something from a charity shop or from Valentino, do what you're doing. Do it good.

MAKE-UP

Since people always ask me, I've asked my make-up artist, Andrew Gallimore from CLM, to let you guys into some of my make-up secrets. This is just for you, though – don't tell anyone…!

EYES: 'After curling Jessie's lashes, I apply a wash of a neutral cream eyeshadow all over the eyelid. I then use a soft brown or grey kohl pencil and sketch along her top lash-line, into her socket and on the outer third of her bottom lash-line, then blend them all with a soft brush. I add a darker colour for definition at the lash-line and depth of the socket-line. Then, using a black liquid liner, I draw a black flick along the top eye-line. At this point I'll maybe add a false lash or just apply a couple of coats of black mascara to Jessie's lashes, and finally line the inner eye with a soft kohl pencil in black for a real sexy finish.'

BROWS: 'Jessie has great brows, but we do like to darken and define them slightly with a dark brown gel liner.'

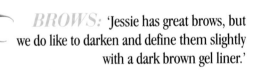

SKIN: After moisturising first, I use a fluid foundation, with not too heavy a coverage, and buff it lightly over the centre of Jessie's face, blending outwards. Her skin is great, so I never need to use much product. I'll add a small amount of light-reflecting concealer under Jessie's eyes, then lightly powder the T-zone with a translucent powder.'

CHEEKS: 'I like to highlight the tops of Jessie's cheeks with a creamy, champagne-coloured shimmer to work with the light, then I add a subtle contour under Jessie's cheekbone and maybe a subtle, natural blush over the apple of her cheek. Most important is that I slightly exaggerate her two beauty marks on her right cheek.'

LIPS: 'I'll always line Jessie's lips with a pencil to give the lipstick longevity and define her perfectly rounded cupid's bow. Then I fill the lips with lipstick, mostly matte in texture, often bold in colour, sometimes nude and natural. For special occasions, we'll often stick a Swarovski Crystal or two somewhere to catch the light for a bit of magic on stage.'

HAIR

*Most of the time I do my own hair and make-up.
When things are too busy, though, Lyndell Mansfield
of CLM is the woman.*

THE FRINGE: 'This is something
that happened the first time I went to see
Jessie. She had a fringe that was wider than
she wanted and needed to grow it out. So
we made a feature of the sides and created
a step on the pieces we wanted to grow out,
and it got a lot of attention. We have since
made it wider again. I am very pedantic
when it comes to getting the fringe right.'

THE BLACK BOB: 'Jessie's main look really suits her. She is great at doing her
own hair, and when I met her she was also used to trying different things with her hair.
The most important thing to me was to create the ultimate bob with an impeccable shine.
The colour helps with the shine and we use different products to achieve it too. We have also
mixed it up a little and done asymmetric versions of the bob to put a modern spin on
a classic, timeless hairstyle.'

THE LONGER, SOFTER LOOK:

'This was first created for the *Glamour* Awards. It was an idea Jessie and I discussed to show that she was more than just "the bob". It has since become a look we love to play with, and by adding extensions and trying different textures and curls we have had many variations. Jessie can pull off just about anything. It's nice to see her in a look that is very red carpet. That first time, a lot of people didn't even recognise her, but now it's expected that she will have a different look and that look is always determined by what she will be wearing and the occasion.'

THE SHORTER, CURLIER LOOK:

'We wanted something fun and playful. It's done on Jessie's regular length and it's a nice way to give her a look without her fringe. Jessie's hair naturally has a wave in it, so we build on it with a curling iron or styler. It's great to see it look so full. It's very different to the straight graphic bob and long hair. We had tried it a few times before it was seen on *The Voice*, at different shows. How the hair looks is always down to the discussion we have once we know what Jessie is wearing.'

NAILS

Jenny Longworth of CLM **takes care of my nails.**

THE FIRST NAILS:

'I saw the "Do It Like A Dude" video and wanted to work with Jessie so badly. The first nails we did were black with gold studs down the centre for "Price Tag".'

'NOBODY'S PERFECT':

'For the "Nobody's Perfect" video, the inspiration for one scene was Salvador Dali's dripping clocks painting, *The Persistence of Memory*. So we wanted to do an exaggerated 3D nail art for it. I decided to get all the inner mechanisms from a clock or watch and put them on the nail. I thought it would be easy; as it transpired, it wasn't. It turns out that watch parts are really hard to get hold of – they're the most expensive part of a watch. I could have bought an antique watch and smashed it up, but that seemed like sacrilege.

'After searching all over London, right at the last minute I decided to go to a charity shop up the road from where I live, and there was an old alarm clock for £2. I got a hammer and smashed it up, and that's where the pieces came from. I stuck on some gold balls with acrylic and the hands of the clock were sticking out, so it was pretty lethal.'

TODAY'S SHOOT:

'For the shoot today we wanted to keep it classic, iconic Jessie, so it's one of her favourite golds and then we'll do a nude later on – simple but effective.'

present

Jess

live in lo

the
VOICE

CHAPTER EIGHT

'In the blink of an eye, I was falling from the sky...'

LaserLight

Make me turn my chair...

STAR TO STAR-MAKER

I was very shocked but honoured to be asked to do the debut series of *The Voice UK* at such an early stage in my career. I'd only had one album out and in comparison to Will.i.am, who has such a long history with the Black Eyed Peas, Tom Jones, who's been around since forever, and Danny O'Donoghue from The Script, who has been in the industry for over ten years, I did worry I would feel slightly out of my depth.

When I started on *The Voice*, I told the producers that I was bound to know people from being on the same circuit earlier in my career; I knew Vince's face and Jay Norton and a couple of others. I've been on the British music scene for years, so there were going to be people that I'd recognise, and I wasn't going to pretend that I didn't know

them, because it would look fake.

What's hard about this industry is that you never know what you're going to be good or bad at until you do it. I didn't know if I was going to be a good coach, and I probably don't know even now. I just had to dive in and do it and hope for the best.

At the same time, the show is called *The Voice* – that's one thing I know I can do. The amount I can sing is down to the fact that I know what I'm doing. I can sit and talk about singing for hours. So when they offered me *The Voice*, I thought, why not? It's a risk. I love a risk.

NEXT UP TEAM JESSIE

I got to work with some incredible artists, my final ten were so much fun and taught me so much about myself as an artist and a person.

I felt so humbled that they wanted to learn from me and take advice from me. Vince Kidd, Becky Hill, Cassius, Toni Warne, Ruth-Ann, Pixie and Indie, Ben, Jessica, Kirsten and David were so wonderful to work with. All of their auditions just sparked something inside me, whether it was tone, diction, range, flourishes or knowing I would be able to better their voices with vocal tricks I knew, I was so excited to work with them all.

I also worked with a brilliant crew at the BBC and I experienced something in life that was completely different. Plus, a lot of people got to hear me sing who hadn't heard me before. My music reached a whole new audience through *The Voice*.

I really did enjoy it, it was so brand new to me to do something that was completely different from what I was used to doing every day – being in front of the stage instead of on it.

NOWHERE TO HIDE

I also believe that people got to see a side of my personality that they didn't know existed. Whether they liked it or not.

I think sometimes my seriousness got mistaken for grumpiness or rudeness, most of the time I was just tired. Or needed a wee. Especially on the live shows. We couldn't go to the toilet the whole show. Tom and I would laugh all the time about that. With the pre-recorded shows, they saw me being silly and funny, because when they edit TV they always want those bits. When it's live, what you see is what you get, and I'm a bit more serious overall because I take singing very seriously, with moments of silliness. I am so focused when I am at work and I get so passionate about singing and music.

With live TV, you hope to be funny, you hope you don't come across as miserable. There was one week, I think Week Three of the live shows, when people said I didn't seem myself. Maybe I'd had a bad day? You know what I mean? When you're on live TV, you can't always be the person everybody wants you to be.

Whatever you do – especially when it's something like *The Voice* – people will always see you how they want to see you. Their brain will always pick out certain things, and they'll see you as a bitch, they'll see you as a diva, they'll see you as the funniest person they've ever watched, they'll see you as charismatic, they'll see you as ugly, they'll see you as beautiful... it's just how they see you. You can't read into it too much, you've just got to focus and know yourself.

It still makes me laugh now that the people who tell you to ignore bad press are always the same fans and 'friends' tweeting you links to the articles.

One big story was that I had ignored the BBC Controller, Danny Cohen. He wasn't even there the day I was supposed to have done that. We've been out to dinner, we're cool, and he came into my dressing room all the time, so it's very weird the papers could create something out of nothing. WHAT? The papers creating something of nothing? NEVER! It is what it is. Nothing new!

> **WITH LIVE TV,** you hope to be funny, you hope you don't come across as miserable

My performance on **The Voice USA.**

THE FANTASTIC THREE

I've loved getting to know Danny, Tom and Will, the crew and my artists. I've really loved being on their journey and having them join mine.

TOM JONES: I love Tom. He is actually a legend. You know what I love about Tom? I'm real with him, and I think that's what he respects about me. I talk to him like he's a normal person. A lot of people act very weirdly around him, very 'Sir Tom'. I said to him, 'I'm not calling you Sir Tom. Can I call you Tommio?' I'd say I'm like his granddaughter.

We did a performance of 'Mockingbird' together for Radio 2 and afterwards we went for dinner to Hakkasan in central London. We just chilled, and talked about *The Voice*, his life, LA, London and music. He was telling me about how he was outside of his house in LA once, just getting his newspaper, and one of those 'star tour' buses went past and all he heard through a megaphone was 'Tom Jones!' He's a warm, funny, lovely person who has some incredible stories. When you get to meet someone like Tom, who has worked with the best, you feel privileged to be able to spend time with him.

DANNY: I'd always liked The Script's music, so I was looking forward to meeting Danny. He's pretty much exactly what you see on TV. He is the sweetest guy and he's very funny. He laughs at his own jokes! He's really honest, he has a big heart and he loves to learn. He's so interested in people and music and who's doing what. He loved doing *The Voice*. I'd be very surprised if Danny didn't come back for a second series. He bought me this nail jewellery. So sweet.

WILL.i.AM: Will's like Stewie, the baby from *Family Guy*. Whenever Holly Willoughby would say, 'Will, over to you', there would be a pause, and you'd wonder what he was conjuring up in his mind. He's the most hard-working, eccentric character and I have the utmost respect for him. Like me, he's very emotional, and he very much wears his heart on his sleeve. He's as honest with me as I am with him, which I respect. I'm definitely planning on working with him, whether that's on his album or mine or for other people. I can't wait to get into the studio with him. He has a warm and very genuine soul.

I think all of us – and this is genuine – will be friends for life.

YOUR HOSTS FOR THE EVENING...

HOLLY WILLOUGHBY: Holly is lovely. She's always very nervous, though you'd never be able to tell. She puts so much effort into what she's doing; it's not just about turning up in a nice dress and reading words from the autocue. She's incredibly professional and always works super-hard to be the best she can be. Also, considering she's had a baby, her body is ridiculous. I definitely didn't realise how beautiful she is until we worked together on the show. She's really sweet and you can see on TV that she's just a normal, down-to-earth woman.

REGGIE YATES: Reggie and I said the other day that we have never spent more than literally thirty seconds together, but we do talk a lot. I think during the show people think we all hang out and have lunch, but he's doing his thing, I'm doing mine, I'm getting ready, he's getting ready. I've known Reggie for a few years. Reggie was there doing the Radio 1 chart show when I went to number two with 'Dude' and number one with 'Price Tag'. Before that, I knew him 'cos he does a night called Trading Places, which I used to go to, and just through the industry generally. He is a real sweetheart, he'll always ask how you really are. Very caring, and he brought some serious style to *The Voice*.

TYPICAL TIME AT *THE VOICE*

Every day for around six weeks we would be at Elstree Studios to film for *The Voice,* usually for around twelve hours. I would arrive early in the morning, around 9am, I would have breakfast, and then look at styling for the week.

I would start with a meeting with the producers to discuss the objective for the day. I'd always like to say hello to everyone – whoever was around. I like the family vibe. Then we'd have to do all the filming for the VTs which were the longest part of all the filming. VT means… I don't know what it means. LOL! Victorious Tulips? Vein Teletubbies? It was all the filming shown between the performances; all the interviews, all the rehearsing around the piano etc. It was hours of filming. We'd have lunch, sometimes on set, sometimes on the go, because we'd be over-running a lot of the time. My team always made it fun when we had long days.

For the live shows, I would have to get there at 10am and I wouldn't leave until midnight, so it was a very long day. We'd have a briefing, when we'd talk about everything that was planned for that night. We'd then go and watch the VTs of all the stuff done during the week. No joke – they film for about eight hours and they use maybe two minutes of it. It's crazy, the amount they film compared to the amount they use. After that, it would be time to rehearse our artists' performances with all the set and lighting. When we came back from rehearsals, I'd get ready. That was always interesting. We did such different looks for every show. I loved having the opportunity to switch it up, keep it fresh. I was never late on set for live shows! I was so proud of myself, as the days were jam-packed and I wasn't often given much time to get ready, so me and my team were always go, go, go!

It's constant when it's live. I like the fact that we're live be-cause as soon as something hap-pens, it's out there. When we

> **I ALWAYS LOVE LIVE TV, BECAUSE IT'S THERE AND IT'S IN THE MOMENT"**

were doing the pre-recorded shows, you'd say something that you maybe shouldn't have, and then you'd have to wait three weeks for the show to come out, so it lingered in your mind. If you just do it and it happens, it's done and it's over. I always love live TV, because it's there and it's in the moment, and everyone's amped for it. I think everyone works harder too, because it's live. The pressure when it's live, knowing it's live, is something that is always in my mind. There's always room for error and you have to learn how to deal with it. I hope I've instilled that in my team. But pressure is a good thing and can make you incredible.

Doing the live group performances was another challenge. It was such a buzz though. Obviously, we're all wearing in-ears so we can hear the music and each other. When I did my group performance my pack for my in-ears wasn't turned on, I remember thinking, 'S***! What am I going to do?!' All I could do was explain to the audience watching live at home what was happening and start again.

I did it because I like to be professional, and I didn't want my group to remember the performance being started badly by me. It actually relaxed them all as it made them laugh. The reaction of me starting again was very mixed. That word 'diva' popped up again but, hey, I'm still singing into my mirror.

If you'd have seen me backstage before the first live episode, I was literally hyperventilating, I was so nervous. I got used to it after a while – you forget you're being filmed and just go with it.

I learnt so much about myself doing *The Voice*, and it was really fun to be a part of the original and debut series.

"BEFORE THE FIRST LIVE SHOW, I WAS LITERALLY HYPERVENTILATING, I WAS SO NERVOUS"

CHAPTER NINE

MAKING HISTORY

'Just be true to who you are...'

Who You Are

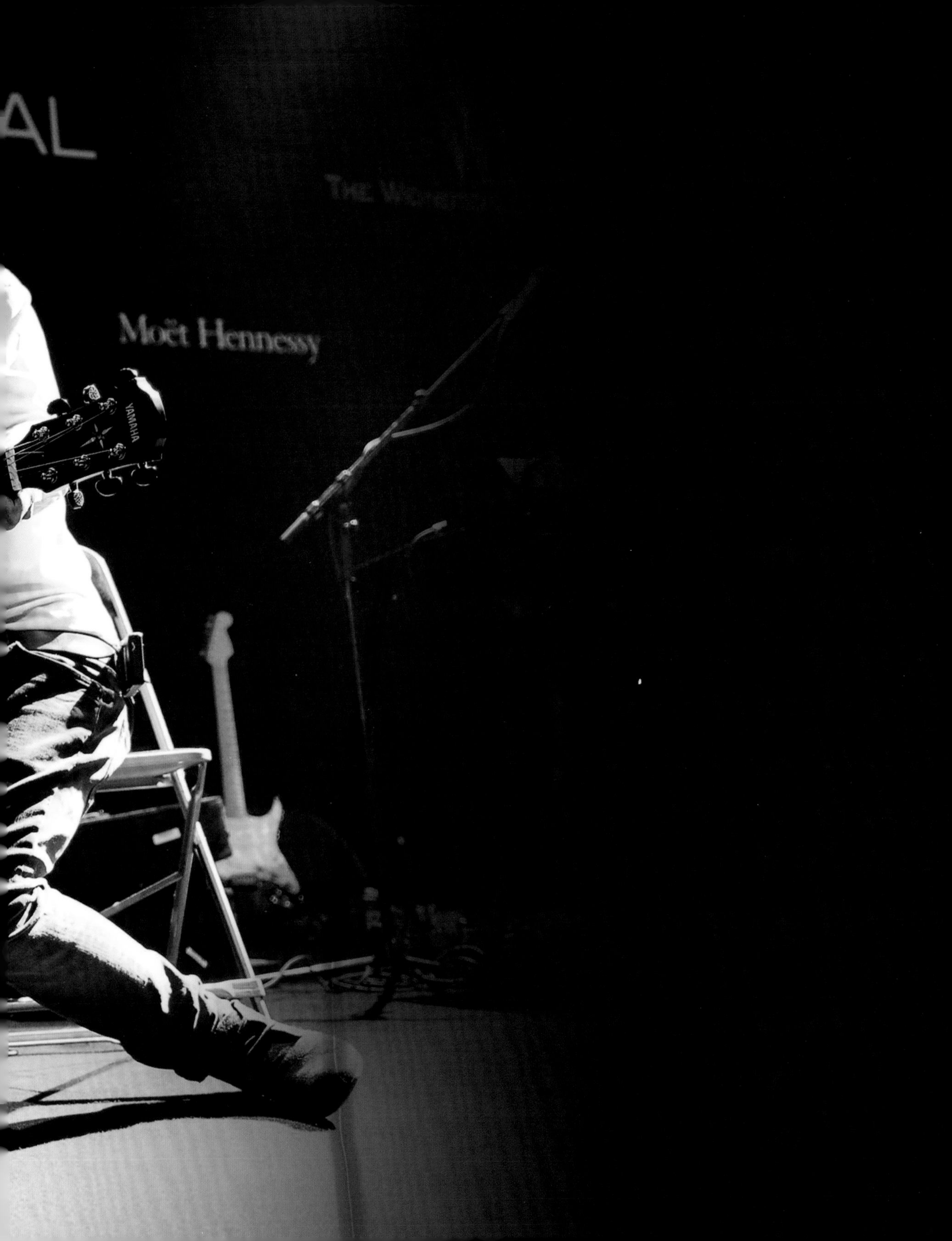
Moët Hennessy
YAMAHA

As well as an incredible 2011, 2012 has been another amazing year. I had no idea that things could spiral even higher. From 'Domino' going to number one to 'LaserLight' breaking records, announcing my headline arena tour and doing *The Voice*, it has been quite a year. Especially when you consider I've still only had one album out.

Then there was the Diamond Jubilee and, more recently, the honour of playing at the Olympics. One of the things I love about my job is the unpredictability. You hope one day for BRITs and Grammys and number ones, but never do you consider all of the other incredible things that can happen. Who knows what else the future will hold but, so far, this has been a dream come true.

MAKING HISTORY

ALBUM TWO

I'm still in the process of album two, still writing and exploring it. I don't want to say what I want it to be and what I think it will be, as who knows – it may end up being completely different. I just want it to really showcase my voice and have great, timeless songs. I am so excited about album two and having new material to share with the world. I will work so hard on making it something I love, but something I know my fans will enjoy too. I love the unknown and the mystery of music.

THE JUBILEE

Being asked to perform at the Diamond Jubilee was massive. I received a letter from the Queen's PA and, let's face it, that doesn't happen often. I had finished *The Voice* final on the Saturday so I was already on a high from that. Then we did the soundcheck on the Sunday, in pouring rain, in five layers of clothes. Will and I were huddled under a brolly; the show was the following day and luckily the weather held out.

When I watch it back, the only thing I notice is how happy I look. Will.i.am was so happy to be there too. We both look like over-excited kids at a party, bouncing around. Seeing The Mall filled with joy and people waving flags is a vision that will never fade from my memory. Seeing my family in the audience was tummy-turning. Everyone was beaming with happiness and pride. It was sensational.

"I WAS SO INTRIGUED TO ASK HER WHAT WAS IN HER HANDBAG"

I met Prince Charles, William, Kate, Harry, and of course the Queen. It's very surreal, because however much she is the Queen, she's still a normal, elderly woman. I wanted to give her a cuddle and a cup of tea. I was so intrigued to ask her what was in her handbag. Smints or Polos? Lip balm? Tissues? Does she have a mobile? Instead, I shook her hand politely and kept quiet. Probably the best option.

I was very, very honoured to be a part of it, and to be representing the younger generation of the UK's music scene. Anything that brings the world together like that, I'm down for it. It was a very positive, happy day, and incredible to share a stage with artists such as:

GRACE JONES
STEVIE WONDER
ANNIE LENNOX
PAUL McCARTNEY
ROBBIE WILLIAMS
ELTON JOHN
TOM JONES
KYLIE MINOGUE

Kylie Minogue was a dream. I never imagined two years into my career would I be asked to do an event so prestigious for the UK and its history.

THE OLYMPICS

I could barely digest the fact I was asked to be a part of the closing ceremony for the London 2012 Olympics. To be asked not only to represent your own country on such a memorable day, but to represent an event that only happens probably once in your lifetime, on your doorstep... The more I think about it, in fact, it's epic. I had again been asked to be a massive part of this country's history.

By the time this book is published, the Olympics will be over and I will have done my performance (hopefully without tripping over or falling off the stage!). Every time I think about it at the moment I get butterflies – you know when you're that nervous about something, and the energy doesn't leave your body, even when you're not thinking about it. It's just constant, excited nerves.

When the Olympic Committee asked me, I almost didn't believe them so I asked to see them, to be sure it was for real. I am one of three current artists on the night – myself, Tinie Tempah and Taio Cruz. The rest of the performers are real legends in the game. I was also the only artist asked to perform twice (pressure) – once with Tinie and Taio doing 'Price Tag', 'Written In The Stars' and a cover of 'We Should Be Dancing' by the BeeGees, and the second performance with Queen – WOW! – singing 'We Will Rock You'. Freddie Mercury was a legend. Big shoes to fill.

Even as I type this, it's still top secret, oooooohhh! We will be rehearsing in silence in Dagenham in a few weeks. We'll be there, singing silently, wearing headphones, so there won't be a chance that anyone passing outside would know what is going on. I feel like I'm part of some sort of secret club. It's a huge event, when the eyes of the whole world will be looking to the UK to show them how to party, and to be asked to represent our country as a closing performer at the Olympics... Well. I won't let you down, pinky swear! Not bad for a girl from Seven Kings!

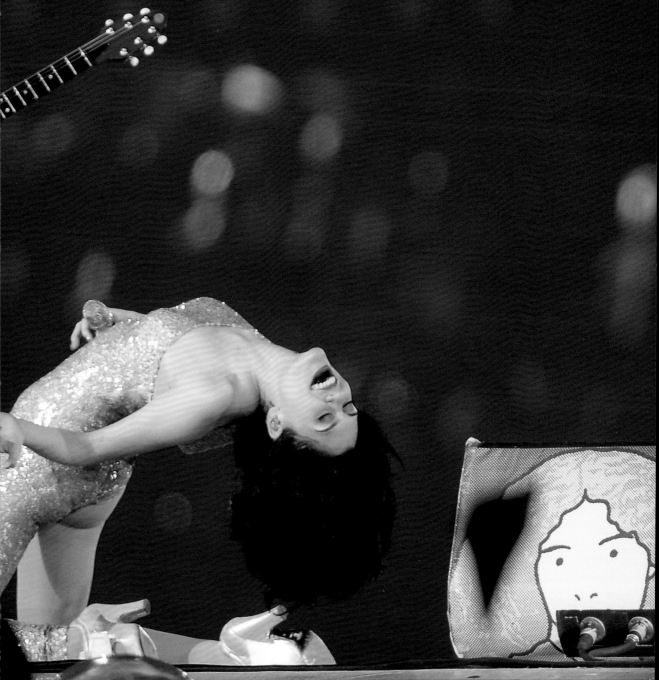

CHAPTER TEN

THE FANS

'You're like a laserlight burning down, burning down on me // You make me feel good // You make me feel safe // You make me feel like I can live another day...'

LaserLight

They pump the life into the heart to keep it alive. Which is why I call my fans Heartbeats.

NUMBER ONE
FAN

I have always said without fans my career wouldn't be possible. I could sing to empty venues and make albums but if no one buys them or comes to my shows to support them then it wouldn't happen. They pump the life into the heart to keep it alive, which is why I call my fans Heartbeats.

I try and have the healthiest relationship with my Heartbeats that I can. A mutual understanding that I will always work hard for my fans as they are always there for me.

Giving them an insight to me as a person, but mainly through my music.

I loved seeing my fan base grow. Until about eighteen months ago I would run my Myspace, my Facebook and my YouTube page. I would get so excited to see the views and numbers increase. It's such a buzz when you know people are starting to talk about your music, something you have worked on for so long.

Getting recognised was surreal and

something I still can't get used to now. My friends and I would play a game, and go to Westfields and guess how many people would recognise me.

I do miss the days of always being able to stop for a photo, as only a few people would know me two or three years ago. I see people get so angry with me now if I can't stop. It's usually only because time doesn't permit me to have a picture with everyone, and more often than not if I stop for one fan then a crowd begins to gather around and I just end up feeling bad. I always stop for my fans when I can, it's so nice meeting different supporters from all over the world who have come together through my music.

When I broke my foot, it was the first chance I had to really read my fan mail and sign some letters and pictures. I replied to over 6,000 letters. It kept me busy and it was so nice to give back to the people supporting me.

> ❝ I ALWAYS STOP FOR MY FANS WHEN I CAN, IT'S SO NICE MEETING DIFFERENT SUPPORTERS FROM ALL OVER THE WORLD ❞

I have two books at home filled with fan letters, cards and notes I have been given over the last two years. I love making memory books, so I can show them to my children one day and always have them as a reminder. I love reading the letters and seeing how different and vast my fan base is, from 6-year-olds who are obsessed with 'Price Tag' to the 40-year-old woman who finally left her house for the first time in nine years after hearing 'Who You Are' – because after years of bullying she felt that she could get her life back. It's so inspiring and so interesting to get to know my fans.

It's amazing what fans do for you, and the effort they go to to support you. Travelling, sleeping outside the venue to be first in line. They make me books and cards, and buy me gifts... It's so generous.

HAIR RAISING

I met a girl through the When You Wish Upon A Star charity called Amy, just after I had surgery on my ankle. She was seventeen and we spent a few hours together in her hospital room in GOSH. I was talking to her about charity and how I want to raise money for equipment etc. We were talking about what I could do, and she said, 'You should shave your head.' Well that was that, it was in my mind and has been now for nearly a year.

It was in August last year that I first spoke about wanting to do it in an interview. I know everyone is waiting, but I have been planning how to make it big, in order to raise as much money as possible. I am in talks now and will be announcing it very soon!

It's so important to give back, and as a celebrity I always want to be helping in any way I can for a good cause. I can't wait to shave my head – so many of my fans said, 'No, don't do it, we love your hair!' But it's just hair, I'm

> **" IT'S JUST HAIR, I'M LUCKY THAT MINE WILL GROW BACK "**

lucky that mine will grow back. If I can save some lives then that's all that matters.

My performance at the amFAR benefit in 2011, where they raised almost $5 million – more than ever before.

THE BEAUTY OF
FAME

I go to many different hospitals and visit wards and, in particular, I go to Great Ormond Street quite a lot. I went fairly recently to record something for Channel 4's Comedy Gala and went to see some kids in the psychiatric unit and various other wards. Visiting the psychiatric unit at GOSH was so emotional, I just wanted them to see me as someone just like them and know they were special to me. It's an honour to know visiting these kids makes them happy.

I sat and spoke to them, asked them questions and wanted to get to know them. There was one girl who cried and rocked in the corner the whole time I was there. They asked me to sing 'Who's Laughing Now' and as soon as I started singing the girl who was crying stopped. I was filled with all sorts of emotions, but I just had to pretend I was OK as the doctors looked over in shock. Those moments are surreal but so special.

There was this one mum who followed us around the hospital the whole time and said, 'Please visit my daughter. She's five years old and she's just come out of a coma.'

I walked into the ward where she was – she was so small this girl, so small – and the mum started to cry. She told me that her daughter had been in a major car accident and they didn't know how much brain damage she'd sustained. There was a bandage on her head that said 'bone flap', where I think she must have had some kind of operation on her skull. It was just so, so awful. Everyone in the ward had watched me come in, I was so aware I had to keep myself together in that situation.

The little girl was lying down; she'd come out of her coma after a week, but she couldn't move. Her mum was saying that the last song she'd been listening to before the accident was 'Rainbow', because she's obsessed with me; her nickname is Jessie Flip-Flop because of me. Her mum, dad, all of the family members were there, and as soon as I walked over, she started to flinch. I held her hand and started singing 'Rainbow' and she started to smile on one side of her mouth. Her whole family broke down in tears. Moments like that are so wonderful, but it's overwhelming to realise how I can affect people. I wrote in the memory book her mum had made for her.

When I do those visits, I try not to get emotional because that's not why I'm there. I'm there to cheer kids up, to give them hope; they don't need me being upset and making them scared. I get emotional for the child, and for the family, because it's so sad, but I go to take them some positive energy. I'm there to help them forget about what's going on for just a little while. I need to be strong in front of the kids and their families. With that little girl, though, I walked out and cried so hard. I've learnt how to hold back and not show emotions until I'm away

from the bedside. My niece is the same age as that little girl and I can't even bear to think how hard it must be to see someone so young go through something like that. There have been maybe two moments when I couldn't hold it back, and I've had a cry. But you have to make sure you're not around the child when you let go. It's not fair on them.

I have recently had a lot of people contacting my management from charities that cater for children's last wishes when they have been diagnosed with terminal illnesses. It's probably the hardest type of meet-and-greet to do. I try and give the child the most love and attention I can, and make them feel special. There is no real way of knowing how you ought to act, I just have to be myself. Knowing they wanted to meet me as a final wish can be a lot for my mind and heart to take. But it's wonderful to give someone something great in the last moments of their life.

I met a little boy called Daniel recently, who is seven years old; he had been diagnosed with terminal cancer and had been given weeks to live. I was asked to meet him as his final wish, so he and his family came to see me just before my show in Shrewsbury. We took pictures and talked, and I just tried to make him laugh. He was so

> **WHEN I DO THOSE** visits, I try not to get emotional because that's not why I'm there, I'm there to cheer kids up...

sweet and so shy – his mum had said he had been talking for the whole journey but when he saw me he just got really embarrassed.

I asked if he wanted to watch at the side of the stage and he said, 'YES!' He sat with his dad and his brother and his little sister. I asked if he wanted to sing 'Price Tag' and his reply was, 'No, I want to sing "LaserLight"!' Loved his honesty.

So he did, he came onto the centre of the stage and sang 'LaserLight' with me. I was so aware of how emotional the moment was for his family and for him. I just knelt next to him and tried to make him forget he was in front of 15,000 people. It was so special. He was as special to me as I was to him.

It's one of best things about becoming well known, being able to use fame in a positive light – I have the opportunity to raise awareness on matters that are close to my heart. It's nice for my fans to see me support issues that need a light shone on them or charities that need money to continue. It's so important.

"IT'S A WONDERFUL THING TO GIVE TO SOMEONE SOMETHING GREAT"

One of the things I have always held close to my heart is helping young people feel accepted. It goes back to me being young and being poorly and wanting the artists I listened to to notice me. I can't help everyone, but I do my best to fill the world with good, and I do a lot of charity work in my spare time. I've always got a kick from making people feel better, ever since I was young. I enjoy cheering people up and even as I've got older, it's still a huge part of me now as an artist and in my music. Everything gets put into perspective when you see how sensational these kids are – the way they deal with issues of illness and disease at such a young age. The way they face pain is inspiring, and it's humbling to know my music can help.

CHAPTER ELEVEN

FOREVER AND ALWAYS

'We're the colours of the rainbow, let's share our pot of gold...'

Rainbow

There are many people who have come in and out my life, people who said I had changed when in actual fact it was them who had. But then there are the people who always stay, through it all. Who understand me and love me unconditionally.

These are the people who will be in my life forever...

FOREVER AND ALWAYS

MY PARENTS

My mum is everything I want to be as a mother to my children one day. Her understanding approach and never-ending consideration for others is unquestionable. Her 'I can do this' attitude is infectious and she has always been a strong and very independent woman; she has taught me how to survive in this unpredictable world. My mum is beautiful inside and out, and never for a second has she stopped me from being myself. She has always encouraged me to grow as a woman and appreciate myself in every way.

My dad is the funniest person I know and it's because of his influence that humour is such an important part of my life and my music. His constant appreciation of the beauty of life and the need to see the good in all things in the world is joyous. He is courageous and such a fearless man, and I have always looked up to him to learn how to be just that. Those who know me know how important my mum and dad are to me. Ever since I can remember, they have been there for me every step of the way, holding my hand when I need them to, building a solid foundation of love beneath me

and my sisters. Growing up they made me laugh, they taught me how to care, and showed me how to always remember to live for the moment. They never hid me from the real world, but they always made me feel so protected and safe. They are wonderful in every role they play in their lives – daughter, son, Granddad, Nanny – but most of all they are perfect parents. Just perfect, and I love them more than anything.

FROM MUM AND DAD: We are extremely fortunate to have three beautiful and gifted daughters. As children they were always very close and supportive of each other and remain so as young women, despite all having different lifestyles, pressures and responsibilities. Jess, as our youngest, always presumed she was as wise and as able as her sisters, and they encouraged her in all she did. Jess has always found joy in the freedom of singing, and we are privileged to share in that joy and be part of her journey. We are very proud that we all remain loving and supportive of each other, and Jess is living proof that dreams can come true. Jess has an undeniable talent; she works so hard and is incredibly dedicated to her craft, family, friends and fans. We get a lump in our throats and tears in our eyes when we think of how much she has achieved. We are so proud of our baby girl.

Mum and Dad xx

MY SISTERS

When I look at my sisters I feel an overwhelming rush of pride. I not only have two sisters, but two soulmates who I can share absolutely everything with. We have all grown into such different women, but we all have at our core what our parents gave us, which is loyalty and love. I have always looked up to them and still do; being five and seven years younger than them, I have tried to follow in their footsteps as much as I can.

Rachel is the middle child and always was the rebellious one. She would always teach me to stand up for what I believed in and not to listen to the whispers in the playground, always be the bigger person. She has an absolute heart of gold and there is a never-ending amount of affection that is always there ready and waiting if I ever just need a hug and someone to talk to.

Hannah is the leader, in a good way. She has always shown me how to be driven and how to focus on my dreams and goals. Her heart is fully on her sleeve and she is always there to make me laugh. She has a childish soul but mature exterior, and that's why she makes such an amazing big sister. Hannah is so thoughtful, always putting everyone else before herself.

If I think about it too much I get tearful, but if I can be anywhere near as amazing as you both are at being mothers when I grow up, then I will be happy.

I love you, Hannah and Rachel.

FROM HANNAH AND RACHEL: When asked to put pen to paper to write about our little sis, we got a bit emotional before even writing down a word! We are so proud of her and it is hard to express that without sounding really soppy! From a very young age Jessie set out to achieve her dream. She has worked relentlessly hard, with an uncompromising passion for her craft to achieve just that. Jessie has done this without sacrificing what she believes in and has remained grounded. Our guess is, though, you already know that... What you may not know is that Jessie is a wonderful sister. She has always been there for us and we are honoured to be able to say that we have remained close despite her hectic schedule. Jess is an amazing auntie to our children, and we would like to say on their behalf – thank you for being you. Without meaning to sound indulgent, because we mean it from the bottom of our hearts – Jess is an amazing individual, with a heart to match her talent. Humbling and honest.

Rachel and Hannah x

MY FRIENDS

I have a group of friends who I trust and love, and who understand me. I'm a loyal person and I expect the same from my friends. They know that. Some have known me all through my childhood; they know Jessica Ellen Cornish from day one. Some I have met along the way. When you meet a real, genuine, lovely person who you befriend it's important to hold onto to them because they can be rare to find. Let me now introduce to you my group of friends.

HOLLY: Holly is like my little sister, an amazing dancer who was in The Royal Ballet when I was little. I was always jealous because I wanted to be a ballerina, but I was too tall and lanky.

I was the one at the back with the rose, waving it in the background just to fill space on the stage, and Holly would be at the front doing some epic solo. She is one of the few people who knows absolutely everything about me, and we giggle like little kids every time we are together. Holly is everything you need in a best friend. She is hilarious, kind, thoughtful, fearless, but most of all loyal. I miss her so much when I'm away from home, but when we see each other it's like we were never apart. Holly is everything to me. I don't know where I would be without a friend like her.

FROM HOLLY: Jess is the big sister I never had. I have known Jess literally most of my life. I have a lot to thank her for, she has been a big part in making me the person I am today. When I am having a bad day and feeling sorry for myself, she is the first person to tell me to fix up and she turns my mood around. When we see each other we giggle until we cry. We share the same sense

of humour, which not many people get as it's pretty childish. We nearly always know what each other is thinking, good and bad. Jess works really hard and is constantly on the GO. But she will never, ever forget her friends. I have learnt so much about friendship and life from her, and I am extremely thankful for her unique friendship. I love her more than I love food, and that's a lot. Taaa Daaaa!

CLAIR: Clair is a Zumba teacher; she would have been with me with a rose at the back. HA! Clair has known me since I was little.

Clair says things like 'ultmate', 'juicy', 'dog' and my favourite, 'pure'. Classic. Clair is one of the funniest friends I have. She never fails to cheer me up; her zest for life is so admirable and her belief in love is still to this day something I really adore about her.

FROM CLAIR: Well well well, what can I say about Jessica. Apart from the obvious: talented, beautiful and so on. Since I have known Jessica, which is around twelve years now, she has always been an epic friend. Always honest, whether you want to hear it or not. She is very generous and thoughtful, and she loves to solve people's problems. Jessica has inspired me, and taught me so much about who I am. She will always find the time to listen. I could write so much more, but two things that always come to mind with Jess are: a big pot of moisturising cream and an ultimate, pure, juicy chicken.

OLIVIA: I grew up down the road from Olivia and we used to wear matching Yipee tops from Tammy Girl. Cool! Olivia is so very sweet and is a great listener. We see each other whenever we can and always laugh so much when we have a catch up. I love how focused Olivia is, she knows what she wants and she just goes for it. I love how much she loves life, constantly travelling and making the most of the moment.

She has the best hair ever too. (Well Jel.)

> ## " JESSICA AND I WOULD ALWAYS SPEND OUR SATURDAY POCKET MONEY ON SWEETS "

FROM OLIVIA: Jessica and I would always spend our Saturday pocket money on penny sweets as children and as the years rolled by we would save it, then spend it all in Tammy girl. A memory that will always stay with me, and something we still talk about today, is a night in April 2001. Jessica was staying over and I had a phone call to say my Nanny had died. I was in floods of tears, but she still managed to make me laugh by choking on a Nik Nak.

I have very fond memories of when we were children. Our friendship is based on lots of laughs and a warm understanding of each other. Lots of love Jess. Olivia x

ANGELINA: Angelina is now one of my hair assistants but I met her through another friend. Ange is so positive and is great with advice, she always makes so much time to listen to me when I need a moan or a vent. She has a great balance of maturity and free-spiritedness. She is so enthusiastic about everything, I love that, and she is some sly secret comedian too, always testing me with the one-liners.

*FROM ANGELINA: Over the last four years Jess has steadily become one of my closest friends. She has encouraged me to follow my dreams. One of the best things about Jess is her warm and loving friends and family; you can tell a lot about a person by the people they surround themselves with. She is a lot like a big sister. She has a big heart and always takes care of me. Jess is so strong and driven, I look up to her in so many ways. And she has the most amazing shoes, but unfortunately they are too big for me. *Sobs*.*

CHERISE: Cherise I have known for nearly eight years. We are as mad as each other, rare to find people who get my humour, but she really does. Cherise is an amazing artist, her voice is like when flowers start to bloom. Her determination and upfront fearlessness in life are what really inspire me. I have seen Cherise at her best and worst times, and she has with me. It's so nice to have friends who you can share your bad times with, knowing they will support you and hold your hand, making them good times again. She is so real, and loyal, something I admire about her. She is always honest.

FROM CHERISE: I think you can tell who your real friends are when you're in your darkest hour, and I can honestly say Jessica has been a great friend. I was scared to tell her about my personal problems because her own life is a whirlwind as it is. But she has always made time, and can always tell when something is up – 'Cherise, you're lying. What's wrong? Talk to me.' Her generosity with her time and empathy towards me and others is amazing. She is one of the few people in the industry who I can say is a true GEM, on and off the stage.

I admire her for boldness, tenacity and strength, before and after she became a worldwide established artist. I have been overwhelmed by her support for my own career journey. It's not often that women who do the job she does (on whatever level) will still make an effort to support and celebrate artists like me. She deserves all the success she has because she has truly worked hard for it. She is a gifted and talented individual, mad LOVE.

JENNY: Jenny is my nail girl, but we have become close over the last three years. Jen is so talented and I have had the pleasure of being part of seeing her become more and more successful through her love and dedication to art and beauty in the past few years. She truly deserves all the success she has, as she works her ass off. Jenny is someone who has taught me to toughen up and not take no s*** from anyone. She is great at clearing my head when I'm over-thinking things and showing me a mature way of looking at life. We take the piss out of each other all the time and we laugh constantly. Anyone who knows Jenny knows she is so caring and thoughtful, and we both love Smurfs. Perfect.

FROM JENNY: Working with Jess over the past couple of years has been so much fun. She pushes through boundaries and takes risks, which is what it's all about for me. We have a similar taste in fashion so I can let my creativity flow when creating her looks. She trusts me and has always been respectful and appreciative of my craft. But more importantly, we have the same sense of humour. Jessie gives me belly laughs like no one else. We spend most of our time sending funny animal pictures to each other, which no one else finds funny! Jess gives me the best advice and puts a smile on my face when I'm down; she always makes me see the funny side of things. Oh, and she makes

a mean lasagne! Above all, Jessie is the 'nail icon' who I am proud to call not only my client, but also a true friend for life.

HANNAH: Hannah is in my band and plays keys. Hannah is the wise owl of the group, she has such a young but mothering soul. Her eyes tell you she has really lived, she has friends everywhere and is so loving to everyone. She makes you feel part of her and her family immediately. Hannah teaches me a lot about life and is always up for a party. I love that about her, her energy for life is infectious.

FROM HANNAH: I have been playing keys for Jess for the last two years. What was initially a working relationship quickly turned into a genuine friendship. Jessie is warm, unaffected and, let's not forget, she is absolutely hilarious. As a musician I love playing behind JJ, her raw talent and vocal abilities leave me speechless. I mean this girl can SAAAANG! I have had my far share of tear-filled moments on stage, as a person I love the fact that JJ just lets me be me. I don't have to pretend and I don't have to embellish, I can just be.

ALISHA: Alisha is my hair stylist. She is so girly and cute and loves Hello Kitty. Alisha has really been there for me on the road when it hasn't been easy. She is so calm and caring, and she knows what makes me happy. I love how ambitious she is and I want her to be happy and enjoy her happiness. I love that I have someone as fun as Alisha to share this crazy experience with.

FROM ALISHA: Along with being AMAZINGLY talented, Jess is wise beyond her years. She is always there for a friend in need and gives the best advice. The way she sees the world and always thinks of others, it's inspiring. Her carpe diem attitude is infectious. I didn't go to work expecting to make a great friend – I really can't call my job 'work'. :)

THE BOYS

Then there's Lewis, Ginger and Phil, the BOYS! They are in my band and everyone who meets them agrees with me that they are three of the sweetest, loveliest guys you will ever meet. They are so caring, and I can talk to them about anything, they are great with advice. They make me laugh so much! It's so nice to have them in my life, travelling around the world. It's so important that you share those experiences with people you really care for. Real friends.

FROM LEWIS: Jessie is like no other artist I have ever worked for. I could say so much about how kind, caring and thoughtful she is, but the best description I can give of Jess is that she has become the little sister I never had. Sounds crazy, because we work together, but Jess has made me feel welcome like no other artist has. To be honest though, the best thing about Jess is that she makes me laugh so hard my sides hurt. We act like we are five years old when we are together and I wouldn't change it for the world. Love you, Jess.

FROM GINGER: My don, Jess. The first day I met her in rehearsal she came in with a cheesecake for all the band. That stuck out to me, and told me she's a loving and selfless person. As time has gone on she has proved

she is nothing but that. Jess is the definition of a hard worker and it's a pleasure to be up on stage with her. Amazing ability and talent, she's definitely one of the finest artists I have ever worked with.

FROM PHIL: Jess is one of the funniest people I have ever met. She has a heart of gold, and always looks out for her friends. It has been such a pleasure working with her for nearly two years and she never fails to be supportive and inspiring to me.

For New Year's Eve, my best friends, my sisters and I went to Thailand for a holiday. We went for two weeks and it was brilliant. We were in a private villa, with our own chef and a pool – it was the best holiday I have ever been on. Amazing company and a real chance to let go and forget work for a bit. After the craziness of 2011, being in Thailand with my friends made me feel so peaceful and relaxed. It had been such a mental year, but finally I was able to sit back and consider my achievements and reflect a little bit. I felt like I had the chance to give myself a little pat on the back at last. It was a much-needed break with all my true friends, and it prepared me for the rush of 2012.

What I love about all of my friends is that they're very creative and ambitious. They're busy and so focused, and that's how I like them to be. I like being surrounded by people who inspire me. They are so important to me and without them I don't know what I would do.

SHOUT OUTS

TINIE TEMPAH

Tinie is one of my closest friends in this business. What's amazing about him is that he is always very honest with me. He is unbelievably talented and I am blown away every time I see him perform, the way he has the crowd in awe. The energy he gives in every show is admirable. It's so nice to have someone who understands what you're doing, but who also makes the time to listen and be there to give advice. We got to know each other in a unique way, because we launched at a similar time – as he's risen, so have I. Tinie works his arse off; he's very passionate and he's a great businessman, and he is the best dressed guy in the UK – hands down. But more than that, he's a really, really lovely guy and is hilarious. He never fails to make me smile.

ELLIE GOULDING

She is my Snow White. I am the Witch. It's a blessing when you can share your career with someone who not only wants to know, but who understands. Ellie is my rock in this industry and we help each other with everything, from songs to hair styles on shoots. Ellie is so natural and is one of the loveliest people I know. Simple and beautiful. Her passion for music and creating art is so inspiring. Her wit teamed with how real she is – she will always be in my life. Love my Snow White.

KATY PERRY

I'm lucky to have had some really fun times with Katy Perry. We hung out at the Capital Summertime Ball in 2012 and talked about wigs. As you do. She gave me some great advice about buying a house once. She said, 'If someone can throw a stone and it could hit the house, don't live there.'

After the Summertime Ball, I went bowling with Katy and all of her crew. Then we went to a London club called Mahiki, and left after about four minutes because it was rammed and we were like fish in a fish bowl. On to another club, Cirque, and that was fun. The Wanted and Carly Rae Jepson were there too. Music is great! We were all pretty tipsy that night!

All I can say about Katy Perry is that she's so normal. She's normal and funny, and works so hard.

PROFESSOR GREEN

I love Green, or 'Stephen' as his friends call him. I didn't really know him that well until I went on tour with him and we travelled around Australia. I've never ever met someone as gentlemanly as Stephen is. He's very old fashioned in the way that he's so polite and thoughtful and well mannered. He always talks about his nan. His nan brought him up, and I got to meet her recently – she's really sweet. Another thing I love about him is that he does warm-ups. Before he went on stage, he did a singing warm-up and you don't see that often from rappers. It's the little things you learn about people as you get to know them that end up being the things you like about them most.

TULISA

Tulisa is such a laugh. What I love about her is that she's a risk-taker. From N-Dubz to her own solo material, she refuses to be part of the crowd. I also love that she talks to me on a level. We saw each other in LA once, and the first thing she said to me was 'Babe, have you got a bag I can borrow?' Girl to girl, I've always got her back – with everything. We've both had our experiences of bad press, we've both been under the spotlight on TV shows, so we really get each other.

JASON DERÜLO

Jason is such a wonderful guy, every time we hang out we just end up laughing and being silly. I spent hours with him once after a show in Germany and we just talked about the music playing in the bar, which was awful, pretending it was our own music, it was very funny at the time. I admire his drive and determination through everything he has been through, including some really tough times with his health.

" IT'S THE LITTLE THINGS YOU LEARN ABOUT PEOPLE THAT END UP BEING THE THINGS YOU LIKE ABOUT THEM MOST "

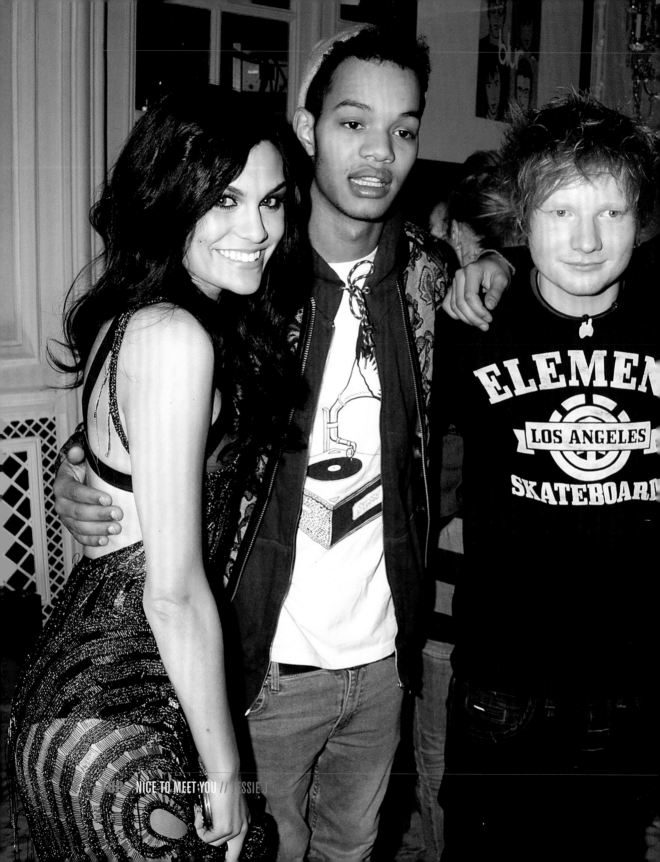

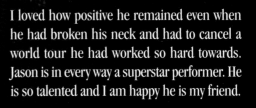

I loved how positive he remained even when he had broken his neck and had to cancel a world tour he had worked so hard towards. Jason is in every way a superstar performer. He is so talented and I am happy he is my friend.

RIZZLE KICKS

Anyone I let lick my face must be OK! Jordan licked my face at the BRITs launch party, so we definitely broke some ice there. Rizzle Kicks are really fun. We've hung out loads and they're really supportive of me and I'm very supportive of them. I remember they did the 'Price Tag' cover and it really got people talking about them. There aren't many British duos any more, and those two are truly original.

ED SHEERAN

Ed was with me on the circuit when I first started doing gigs, so when we see each other we are so normal with each other. He is such a great guy and so humble and so individual. His voice! Heavenly. He just does it and I admire him for it. Yes Ed, so proud of you matey. :)

CHIPMUNK

Chip is so open and wears his heart on his sleeve, as a person and as an artist. I loved watching him break the mould back in the day and he has never stopped pushing and breaking boundaries as a UK rapper, recently jetting to the US and making it happen for himself there. Not many people have the guts to do that kind of thing. I admire him for his ambitious mindset. Chip is great and I really enjoy talking to him, he makes me laugh!

WHAT IS Jessie J LIKE?

WILL.I.AM

Jessie J is one of the coolest, funniest, most energised, sporadic, dopiest singers, hungriest, focused, talented, dopiest vocalists – did I say dopiest singers? – I have met in a long time… She made it amazing and fun to be a part of *The Voice* and I am happy to know her.

REGGIE YATES

I first met Jessie a long time ago – she was in her late teens and had a butterfly drawn in liquid eyeliner on her face. As expected, I questioned it and got suitably shut down by her perfect balance of cheek and charm.

Between the butterfly and the banter, I knew we would get on. When we started working together on *The Voice* I thought she would absolutely nail it, and she did just that. With an incredible hand-picked group of singers on her team she did herself proud across the series, and I hope she never has to give me a vocal lesson, because as a teacher she kicks ass.

MONICA

Clive Davis's pre-Grammy party was my first time meeting Jessie. I loved her personality. She was live and unafraid. She constantly made me laugh, speaking with my Southern accent. Yet she was very professional in her approach to our rehearsals. It was a special moment for us both, especially since it was a tribute to the legendary Ms Diana Ross and Whitney Houston, whom we both love and admire…

Jessie's talents are mesmerising. On a scale of 1 to 10, I give her 1,000. Her vocal ability is not often seen these days. Her writing is young and fresh, yet still touches the depths of your soul. Not to mention her range is sick! She's an all-round beast, to say the least. I was honoured to know she was influenced by me. I can hear things in the soul of her voice and her riffs that feel familiar in a special way.

Without question Jessie J is, and will always be, a global star. Her talent clearly demands that, but also her humility and love for the people is what will carry her forever.

Jessie is a vocal powerhouse. No matter where you're from, the sound of her voice will touch you and move you. Music is the universal language and Jessie J speaks it loud and clear. From the UK to the US, she's loved. She's a star.

CHIPMUNK

Well I fancy Jessie... But so do most guys and girls, LOL. (Make me twenty-five.) What I love about Jessie the most has got to be her unique flair. I don't think there is a singer worldwide that she couldn't riff next to. She beat me to number one, one week, but oh haha! I am still rooting for her through all walks in life. I wish her many more successful and, more importantly, happy years. Big hug, big kiss, Chippa xx!

ED SHEERAN

Jessie is one of the most hardworking and talented people I know in this industry, and it's very rare you get both. A lot of people take the work side of it for granted, but since I've known her I don't think she has had more than two days off.

She deserves everything that comes her way, and I am proud to call her a friend.

JASON DERÜLO

I never had many friends, I have always been a bit of a loner. Jessie was someone that I took to, from the first time I met her after a show in Germany. We talked for a couple of hours and joked as if we had known each other for years. She has such a magnetic personality, our days prove many similarities.

Her fans, family and music remain her life. Every day is spent on cultivating those three things. Being dedicated to something is very different from actually living it. When I broke

> **" JESSIE IS ONE OF THE MOST HARDWORKING AND TALENTED PEOPLE I KNOW IN THIS INDUSTRY "**

my neck, I got messages from press, fans, family, you name it. I didn't feel like anyone truly understood how difficult it was, going through that traumatic experience while under the microscope of the world. No one, but Jessie. You learn through experience and she went through a similar sort of injury situation. Words of encouragement seemed to be more effective from her because she has been in my shoes. I don't know if she even knows how much of an effect she has had on my life in that period or in my life in general. My friend Jessie, or as I call her 'Lil Bit', is a beautiful soul who wishes to inspire and heal through music.

PROFESSOR GREEN

I first met Jessie at T4 Stars of 2011 (we had previously spoken on Twitter, a conversation which I think began with Jessie telling me I had the best teeth in hip-hop and me explaining I'd paid quite a lot for them). A tour of Australia and the odd random crossing of paths later, and I can safely say she's one of the most lovely, down-to-earth and honest artists I've met, she even had a pic with my nan and auntie. She's from east so she was always going to be inherently awesome, but she really is brilliant – not many people would crash the stage during their support act's set dressed as a tiger during a song called 'Jungle'.

TINIE TEMPAH

I first met Jessie very briefly at a party for *RWD* magazine. I was already aware of her music, and a fan. I remember her coming across as very confident and genuine. I felt all of that energy she puts out on stage instantly. Jessie had all of the early signs of a true star. We blew up about the same time, and went through very similar experiences together. I try and do like 'Wow, we went to the BRITs', with as many people in the same situation as I can, to try and help make sense of it all – the crazy things that happen when you experience success. She is definitely one of the main people I do that with, especially about America – all the funny chat shows we've done, and all the weird and wonderful cities and towns we've been to. It's also nice that she's a REAL talent who can go all the way. It almost feels like I'm witnessing the journey as it unfolds. We've had some really good times together. Earlier in 2012, we were all on tour together in Australia and Pro Green was supporting Jessie in Sydney. She came out during his set dressed as cheese, which he apparently has a phobia of. That was quite funny. I think Jessie has blown because she can really sing. There's no denying it. She has all the charisma and star quality that our favourite artists from all around the world possess. She's the finished article. We both keep saying it, but there are most definitely plans to work together. Watch this space!

CHAPTER TWELVE

WHO I AM

'Don't lose who you are in the blur of the stars...'

Who You Are

A few random things that you may not know about me...

JUST JESSICA

I ONCE STUCK A...

Pocahontas stick-on earring up my nose and was taken to the doctor's to have it removed. As you do.

I HAD TO HAVE THE BUTTERFLIES...

of my earrings removed from my earlobes at the hospital when I was eight after having my ears pierced, because I wouldn't leave them alone. I obviously didn't get on with jewellery when I was younger.

ANXIETY DREAMS KEEP ME...

awake at night sometimes. I dream that I have no clothes and have to go on stage naked. Or I forget the words at a show. I suppose I'm an over-thinker, everyone tells me I am. *Thinks some more*.

THE FIRST CAR I OWNED...

was a Ford Ka. It took me five times to pass my test (don't tell anyone) – careful if you see me on the road! I called my car Meg and we were together for three happy years. We had great times and she never let me down. She's in the family still; I couldn't bear to let her go. My dad's got her now, and he washed her the other day with a scourer. She's covered in scratches. He phoned me and said, 'Babe, I've ruined your car.' Trust my dad.

ONE OF MY FAVOURITE MEALS...

is my mum's honey chicken with crunchy fried cabbage and spinach, a jacket potato and corn on the cob with cheese on it. Delicious.

I USED TO EAT MUD...

and ants as a child. Weird, maybe I thought I was a worm?

I'M SCARED OF...

heights, although I'm getting less scared. I can get on a plane now without freaking out but I do get vertigo.

I'M CLAUSTROPHOBIC...

I don't like being in places where I don't see an easy exit.

IF I HAD A SUPERPOWER...

it would be to heal the sick and to fly. To be able to make people better would be cool but then to fly home would be extra cool. Casually just flying around.

ONE OF MY FAVOURITE BOOKS...

is *Charlotte's Web* because it's one of the first books I ever read. It brings back good memories of me managing to get through one book the whole way, and my mum and dad being really proud of me.

I'M OBSESSED WITH...

all things miniature. The thought of a micro pig and a micro horse makes me laugh so much.

THE QUESTIONS I MOST HATE...

being asked are the ones that aren't anyone's business. And 'What's your favourite thing?' and 'Cats or dogs?' and 'Bath or shower?' Why do I have to choose? Why can't I like both?

MY FRIENDS WOULD SAY...

I'm emotional, kind, generous, hardworking, intense, passionate, mumsy and funny. I think.

THE BEST KISS...

of my life was... private.

I'M MOODY WHEN...

I'm either hungry or tired. If I'm both – woah! Just don't come near me.

I'M LITERALLY S*** AT...

everything apart from singing. OK, that's a little dramatic but I can't do maths, I don't think I can ride a bike (well I haven't tried for years), I can't play an instrument, I can't ice skate.

I CAN DRAW...

I got an A in my Art A-level. I love to draw now. Pencil drawing the most.

I HAVE BROKEN...

my little toe twice – once when I was in year 7 and I ran into a tree and then again recently when I kicked my suitcase. Both times it bloody hurt.

I ONCE SPRAYED...

the Sporty Spice deodorant into my eye in Tammy Girl, and it was so bad I was taken to the stock room until I could see.

I STOLE A HOODY ONCE...

from Atlantic Clothing that had 'It wasn't me' written on it, when the Shaggy tune was big. The security didn't find it funny when I said I was joking.

I CAN FIT...

my fist in my mouth. Nice gross one to end on.

My first
performance in LA.

FOCUS
POCUS

DIFFERENT MUSIC FOR DIFFERENT DAYS...

WHEN I NEED A GOOD CRY...

'Love And Affection' by Joan Armatrading. My mum used to sing it to me when I was a kid. If I listen to it, it reminds me of my mum.

THE VERY FIRST RECORD I BOUGHT WAS...

'Brimful Of Asha' by Cornershop – either that or the Hanson album. I loved them, especially the middle brother, Taylor. I was also obsessed with Michael Jackson's nephews, 3T.

THE LAST CONCERT I WENT TO WAS...

Ed Sheeran at Brixton Academy. Anyone who can stand on a stage with just a guitar and some amps, and kill it to the point where the audience is going apes*** – he must be a secret ninja. He writes songs people can relate to and is so talented, his voice just melts you. He's done so well because he's being himself and he's a nice guy. Every time we see each other, we talk about working together; it will definitely happen.

THE ALBUM THAT HAS INSPIRED ME...

the most as an artist is Lauryn Hill's *The Miseducation of Lauryn Hill*. When I heard that album, it made me want to be her. I wanted to write about my life in the way she'd written about hers: 'I was just a little girl / Skinny legs, a press and curl / My mother always thought I'd be a star...'

THE TRACKS THAT ALWAYS GET ME...

on the dance floor are 'I Wanna Dance With Somebody' by Whitney Houston, 'Rude Boy' by Rihanna and 'You're The One For Me' by D. Train. That's a few, it's not hard to make me dance.

A SONG I WISH I'D WRITTEN IS...

'Never Too Much' by Luther Vandross. Instead I cover it on my tour now. Love that song.

MY HAPPY SONG IS...

Beyoncé's 'Love on Top'. Just as soon as it starts, I smile.

THE SONG THAT MAKES ME...

turn the radio up is Michael Jackson, anything MJ!

THE SONG THAT'S MY GUILTY PLEASURE...

is 'Mambo Number Five' by Lou Bega (because it's got my name in it. I was so hyped when that came out, LOL!)

THE BEST GIG THAT I'VE BEEN TO IS...

Beyoncé. Just after Glastonbury in 2011, she did a private show at Shepherd's Bush Empire. There were maybe 600 people and she was like, 'What do you want to hear me sing?' She was incredible and it was a really intimate show. I sat there with my broken foot next to Adele and Tinie and Jay-Z and Gwyneth Paltrow. My foot was well off, boy! But I just couldn't leave. I was in so much pain, because I'd just had my surgery and I had to sit with my foot squashed in between the seats. When I went home, it was three times the size. That said, the show was unforgettable. Beyoncé is just an icon.

JESSIE'S
TATTOOS

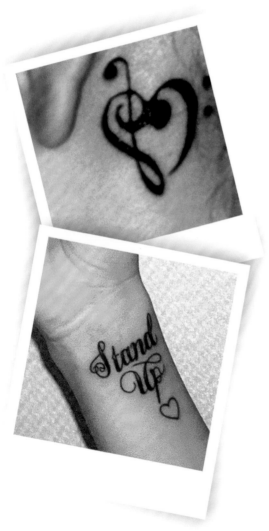

I HAVE FOUR TATTOOS

1 A treble and bass clef behind my ear in the shape of a heart – to represent my love for music.

2 'Stand Up' with a heart on my wrist. I got this on 31 December 2009. To remind myself always to stand up for EVERYTHING I believed in. It was a tattoo for a new me and a new year.

3 'Don't loose who you are in the blur of the stars' – yes it says 'LOOSE', not 'lose'. Only I could get a spelling mistake. My mum told me four days after I had it done, I didn't even notice. LOL! Made me laugh, just taught me never to get a tattoo in Essex again.

Don't get it twisted – I am so proud to be from Essex, it's important to always remember where you're from and represent. We don't all fit the stereotype, and I am just trying to make Essex proud.

4 ?!?!?!?!

WHAT I
LIKE

DIPTYQUE AND JO
MALONE CANDLES
PEPPERMINT TEA
MANUKA HONEY
LIPSTICK
PAMPERING
MYSELF
A GOOD FILM
**CLEAN
HOUSES**
MY HAIR FRESHLY
CUT AND DYED
LINDT CHOCOLATE
MANNERS
JORDANS
(TRAINERS)
**CHRISTIAN
LOUBOUTINS**
POINTY NAILS
A GOOD
PEDICURE
GOOD HUMOUR

MULLED WINE
LOUD MUSIC
FRUIT CIDER
BOWLING
MICKEY MOUSE
DESIGNER
SUNGLASSES
LAUGHING
DEEP-FRIED MARS
BARS
SUNSHINE
SEXY BACKS
SNOW
A GOOD NIGHT'S SLEEP
COOKING FOR MY
FRIENDS
TIDYING AND
SORTING AND
ORGANISING
CUDDLES
TRAVELLING TO NEW PLACES
50p SWEET BAGS
ROLLER COASTERS

WHAT I DISLIKE

GRISTLY MEAT

BAD BREATH
(MAKE SURE YOU FLOSS)

MASTICATION

LIARS

PATCHY FAKE TAN

RAW ONIONS

ZOOS (I DON'T LIKE SEEING
ANIMALS IN CAGES)

FAKE UGG BOOTS

BEING TIRED

WAXING

REALLY LOUD
RINGTONES

CHOCOLATE ICE
CREAM

COFFEE

DIRTY
FINGERNAILS

CHEATERS

MOSQUITOES

SCARY LIFTS THAT
ARE GLASS

TRAFFIC

TURBULANCE

MY PHONE BATTERY
DYING

BEING KISSED BY
STRANGERS

DISLOYALTY

DARK CHOCOLATE

MUMBLERS

Me at the Teenage Cancer Trust concert at the Royal Albert Hall, 2012.

COME DINE WITH JJ

I go in on the cooking. I make my mum's honey chicken but I can't give you my mum's chicken recipe though – that would be sacrilege.

LAMB LASAGNE

INGREDIENTS:

1 onion
2–3 cloves of garlic
lamb mince
1 red pepper
1 green pepper
1 tin of sweetcorn
2 tins of chopped tomatoes
Reggae Reggae sauce
Nando's medium Peri-peri sauce
tomato ketchup
tomato purée
honey
salt and pepper
lemon juice
soy sauce

For the cheese sauce:

a big chunk of unsalted butter
1 cup of plain flour
1 pint of milk
as much cheese necessary to make
it cheesy (save some for the top
though)
salt and pepper
lasagne sheets, either fresh or dry
(but pre-cooked)

METHOD:

This is my very own recipe. HERE WE GO!

First, I fry the onion and garlic until they're soft, then I put the meat in and get that cooked a little bit. Now, make sure you have everything prepared in advance: dice up your pepper (you can also put in some chopped mushrooms if you like); open up your tinned sweetcorn and tomatoes. Fry that up together with the meat and the onions, and then I put in some Reggae Reggae sauce, ketchup, tomato purée and honey. I put honey in everything: I like sweet food. Add pepper, salt, lemon juice – I put that in everything too – then a bit of soy sauce. I get all that going in the pan, bubbling away.

While that's cooking, I start my cheese sauce. You just need to melt the butter, then slowly add in the flour and milk and loads of cheese. Whisk that up and add some salt and pepper. Use an electric hand whisk to make it quicker.

Once everything's cooked, it's time to layer it up. I do the meat, then the pasta, then the cheese sauce, pasta, meat and so on. Make sure you put it in the oven at 180°C for a good 30–45 minutes, because the pasta takes a while to cook. Once it's all brown and bubbling on top, it's good to go. If you want to cook for your friends or impress someone special, I'm telling you, this is tasty and so easy to do. TAAA DAAAAA!

LET'S GET
ORGANISED

Those who know me know I'm freakishly organised, my wardrobe is colour co-ordinated and my kitchen cupboards are like a show room. Haha! My friends take the mickey but the way I see it, an organised life is an organised mind.
So here are my *FIVE TOP TIPS* to getting organised.

THINGS TO DO

IF YOU SEE AN IMAGE...
in a magazine you love, rip it out and stick it into a scrap book. It's a good way to see what you like and what you can save up for as a little treat. I used to do this growing up.

MAKE A LIST...
once a week and keep it in your bag so you can remind yourself of what you need to do. Be your own personal assistant.

KEEP YOUR WARDROBE...
in sections of clothes. So all dresses together, all trousers together etc. It makes it easier to decide what to wear when you're getting dressed.

FIVE THINGS TO ALWAYS...
have in your bag are: a spare charger, hand sanitiser, chewing gum, lip balm and tissues.

ALWAYS KNOW WHERE...
your personal documents are and keep them organised. It's rare that you need them, but good to know they're safe.

LET'S GET
BEAUTIFUL

MY TOP FIVE TIPS IN BEAUTY

WASH YOUR MAKE-UP BRUSHES...

every few days to get rid of dirt residue that you might end up reapplying to your face (YUCK!) You can use shampoo to clean them, and then put your brushes and your make-up into a clear, clean bag so it's easy to find everything.

COCONUT OIL...

is great for your hair and really cheap. Leave it in overnight and then wash it out properly in the morning.

I HAVE USED OILATUM...

since I was little, it's a great moisturiser for all skin types. It's non-perfumed and great for making your skin feel hydrated.

ALWAYS WEAR A SLIGHTY LIGHTER...

shade of foundation if you add bronzer so you are the same colour as your body and not two or three shades darker.

LOOK AFTER YOUR FEET...

A good scrub once a week will prevent hard skin building up.

JESSIE BY
NUMBERS

(AS OF JULY 2012)

1 **RECORD BROKEN** – FIRST FEMALE TO HAVE SIX TOP TEN SINGLES FROM ONE ALBUM

3 **SOLD-OUT** TOURS

4 **COUNTRIES** VISITED IN ONE DAY – ENGLAND, FRANCE, GERMANY, SPAIN

7 **SINGLES** AND VIDEOS RELEASED

14 **ARENA DATES** ON NICE TO MEET YOU TOUR

17 **YEARS OLD** WHEN I WROTE MY FIRST SONG ('BIG WHITE ROOM')

17 **AWARDS** WON

30 **BBM CONTACTS**, INCL. TREY SONGZ, RITA ORA, WILL.I.AM, TINIE, TULISA, TINCHY, CHIPMUNK AND JASON DERÜLO

27 **FAVOURITE** NUMBER

25 **PAIRS** OF SUNGLASSES OWNED

28 **NUMBER** OF MAGAZINE COVERS

42 **HOURS** – THE LONGEST I'VE STAYED AWAKE IN ONE STRETCH; YOU START SEEING SPIDERS THAT AREN'T THERE!

49 **NUMBER** OF MY FIRST HOUSE

0 **TIMES** I HAVE BEEN MARRIED

100 **CD**s OWNED – BUT I DON'T REALLY PLAY THEM; I LISTEN TO EVERYTHING ON iTUNES

250+ **PAIRS** OF SHOES OWNED

70 **LIPSTICKS** OWNED

4,052 AMOUNT OF MOST EXPENSIVE PHONE BILL, IN POUNDS, TO DATE

+

10,498 TWEETS SENT

+

150,000 PEOPLE PLAYED TO, AT A HORSE-RACING EVENT IN DUBAI

5 MILLION + TWITTER FOLLOWERS

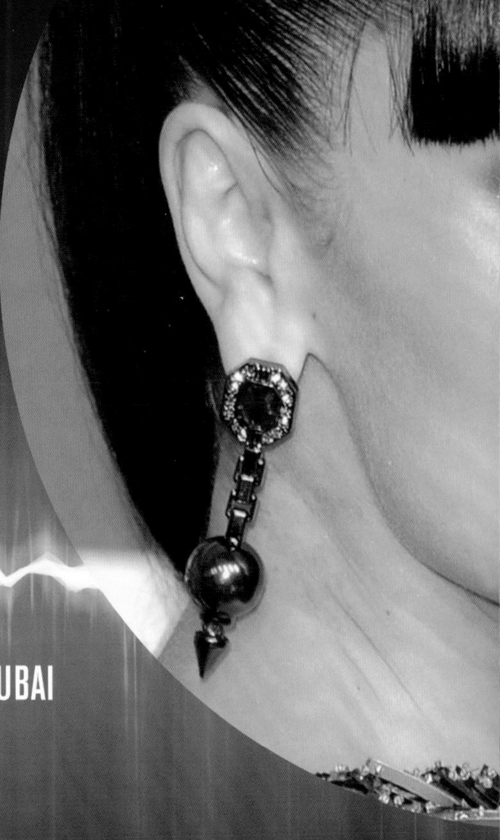

7.5 MILLION ⁺ FACEBOOK LIKES

12 MILLION ⁺ TOTAL SALES

71 MILLION ⁺ VEVO VIEWS

400 MILLION ⁺ YOUTUBE VIEWS

TO
CONCLUDE

Someone said to me the other day, 'If you don't feel that you've got someone to look up to, then be the person for people to look up to.' Be the change you want to see in your life, and be the change you want to see in the world. Even if it's a tiny little thing, leave your mark. Make people remember.

I'm so glad that I took everything on, from the ups to the downs, the bad to the good. It's all been worth it. I could never give up. I can't quit. Quitters don't win and winners don't quit.

When I wrote 'Who You Are', I had such moments of doubt, but music saves me. It really does. It makes life feel brand new.

In some ways, I don't know who I am yet. I think that's why my first album was so interesting. I was talking to my mum and dad about it the other day; I was saying that I don't think that the first album was me going, 'I know who I am.' It was about me embracing all the good and bad of the person I was growing into, if that makes sense. Just be who you are. Just do you, be you. It will all make sense one day.

My life has changed so much from two years ago to now, and will continue to change. I'm constantly evolving and I have to make sure that I'm adapting to change in all areas of my life, work and personal. It's blossoming beautifully.

Coming to the end of the book, it's been really interesting writing it. I've had the opportunity to relive not only the exciting achievements of the last two years, but all of those funny memories of growing up too. Putting the puzzle pieces together and seeing the experiences that made me the woman I am today.

I've suffered a lot of knocks along the way and I've taken some risks, which I believe you have to do in order to become not only a great artist but, also, a rounded person.

Whether you've just joined my journey, or you've been there from the beginning, welcome and let's hope we're all in it forever.

Always dream big, people.

Oh – and it's been so
NICE TO MEET YOU!

PICTURE CREDITS